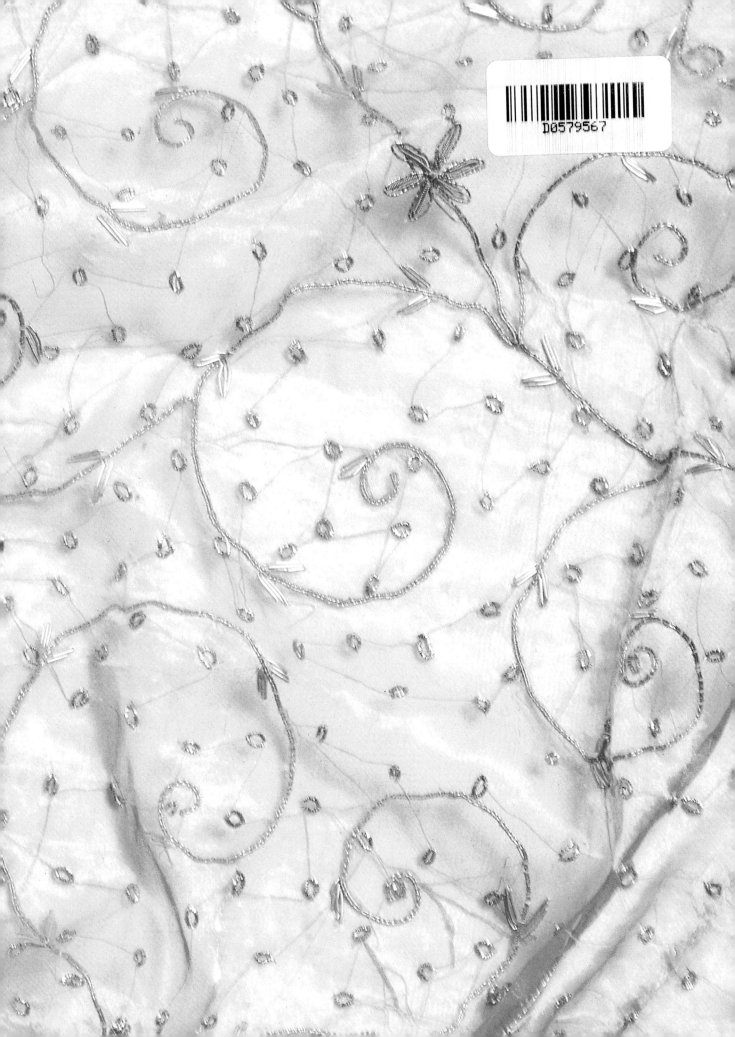

Authentic Recipes from
INDIA

Recipes by Brinder Narula, Vijendra Sanjay Mulkani
and Thomas John

Introductory essays by Jennifer Brennan, Jasjit Purewal
and Karen Anand

Photographs by Luca Invernizzi Tettoni

PERIPLUS

Published by Periplus Editions with editorial offices at
130 Joo Seng Road #06-01, Singapore 368357.
Tel: (65) 6280-1330; fax: (65) 6280-6290.
Email: inquiries@periplus.com.sg
Website: www.periplus.com

Hardcover ISBN: 0-7946-0237-1
Paperback ISBN: 0-7946-0294-0
Printed in Singapore

Distributed by

North America, Latin America and Europe
Tuttle Publishing, 364 Innovation Drive,
North Clarendon, VT 05759-9436.
Tel: (802) 773-8930; fax: (802) 773-6993.
Email: info@tuttlepublishing.com

Japan
Tuttle Publishing, Yaekari Building, 3F
5-4-12 Osaki, Shinagawa-Ku, Tokyo 141 0032.
Tel: (03) 5437-0171; fax: (03) 5437-0755.
Email: tuttle-sales@gol.com

Asia Pacific
Berkeley Books Pte Ltd
130 Joo Seng Road #06-01, Singapore 368357.
Tel: (65) 6280-1330; fax: (65) 6280-6290.
Email: inquiries@periplus.com.sg
www.periplus.com

All recipes were tested in the Periplus Test Kitchen

Photographer: Luca Invernizzi Tettoni

Food stylists and recipe testers: Brinder Narula,
Vijendra Singh, Sanjay Mulkani and Thomas John

Introductory essays co-written by Jennifer Brennan
and Jasjit Purewal, except where noted.

Contents

Food in India
Three thousand years of tradition and astonishing variety

India is a vast and ancient land, its recorded history dating back over three thousand years. Yet India today, despite its deeply rooted traditions, is the product of centuries of change—new ideas, new faiths and new products arriving with traders and invaders—with colonizers, and with immigrants fleeing repression elsewhere. The result is a rich tapestry of contradictions and contrasts that never ceases to fascinate.

The astonishing variety of India is reflected in its cuisine, which is regarded by those who have enjoyed genuine Indian food as being among the world's greatest. Like the overall fabric of the land itself, the cuisine of India is the result of countless historical, religious and regional influences.

Stretching from the snowy mountains of Kashmir down to the southern tip of verdant Kerala, from the harsh deserts of Rajasthan in the west across to the remote tribal regions of Assam on the Burmese border, India encompasses an enormous variety of climates that naturally influence the produce available. The Kashmiris, for example, are largely meat eaters since agricultural produce is limited in mountainous regions. In coastal Kerala, where fish abound in the Arabian Sea and "backwaters" that weave through coconut groves, fish and rich coconut milk curries predominate.

Religion and caste also play their role in influencing India's cuisines. This is the land which gave rise to two of the world's major religions, Buddhism and Hinduism, and also produced Jainism and Sikhism. Faiths from other lands—Islam, Christianity, Zoroastrianism and the Bah'ai faith—have also taken root in the subcontinent. Religious strictures dictate that certain people will not eat beef or pork, while others are strict vegetarian.

Yet despite the many differences of religion, caste, community and class, there are enough common elements which make it possible to define Indian cuisine. The basis of an Indian meal is a grain, which may be rice, wheat, millet or corn, depending on the region. This is generally eaten with lentils or beans (dal), vegetables and savory pickles or chutneys. Other dishes of fish, meat or poultry may be added, as well as yogurt. Invariably, lentils, vegetables and other dishes will be seasoned with spices which not only perform miracles in transforming the taste of the food and sharpening appetites jaded by the heat, but have medicinal values which were recorded in religious texts some three thousand years ago. Cooking and eating Indian

cuisine is thus a discovery of the culture, the richly varied history and the spicy treasures of this fascinating land.

Tastes from a Varied Subcontinent
India is a land of amazing variety, beginning in the awesome Himalayas in the north and moving on to the great Gangetic plain with its immense and sacred waters, down through the harsh but strangely beautiful deserts of Rajasthan, through plateaus and thick forests, through the Punjab (the "Land of Five Rivers") to the lush green splendor of Kerala—a distance of more than 1,800 miles.

With its vast land area, India naturally encompasses an enormous variety of climates. As well as its distinct seasonal cycles, India has numerous religions, races and ethnic landscapes which turn the subcontinent into a jigsaw of small nations, resulting in a culinary kaleidoscope as colorful as any glass mosaic adorning a Mughal palace.

Generally speaking, rice and wheat are the main staples of the Aryan-influenced north; however, the desert lands of Gujarat and Rajasthan depend far more on millet and corn. In the extreme north lies the fairy tale land of Kashmir, where racial origins go back to Persia and Afghanistan. Nestled in the Himalayas, Kashmir, with its almost legendary beauty of crystal clear lakes and snow-clad mountains, depends largely on the valley of Srinagar for agricultural produce. Fruit and nuts are the only real crops of Kashmir, so both Hindus and Muslims depend on a diet rich in meat. Kashmiri food is characterized by its subtle blending of fragrant spices (especially the world's most

expensive spice, saffron), by its richness (often the result of ground nuts or poppy seeds) and by the use of asafoetida, a resin that adds a distinctive flavor and is also believed to aid digestion.

Some of the most popular Kashmiri foods include lamb marinated in yogurt; mutton slow-cooked in milk and scented with nutmeg; Roghan Josh, a rich meat curry; and the famous Goshtaba or meat loaf, cooked for many hours to an inimitable silky chewy texture. Kashmiri weddings are incomplete without Mishani or the "seven courses of lamb," a paradisaical spread for meat eaters. A variety of leavened and unleavened breads are an essential part of any Kashmiri meal.

The Gangetic plain in the middle and eastern part of India is both a rice and wheat-eating belt, although millet and corn are used in some areas by the lower–middle classes. The normal meal in this region consists of plain rice accompanied by vegetables stir-fried with spices, *dal*, unleavened bread (either dry-fried on a griddle or deep-fried in oil), plain yogurt and a milk based sweet. Chutneys and pickles are common accompaniments,

while fruit is enjoyed in season. Meat and fish are consumed mostly by the more affluent middle class and are not a regular part of the diet, except in the east and northeast.

The east, with its proximity to the Bay of Bengal and its numerous ponds and rivers, is where fish consumption is highest. This is the only part of India—with the exception of the Kerala coast—where fish is the most popular food. East Bengal (now Bangladesh) prefers its fish from large rivers, while the west, with Calcutta as its nerve center, gets its seafood from estuaries and ponds. Hilsa, a type of shad which is a member of the herring family, is the most popular fish in the region, despite its numerous small bones.

West Bengal is known for its use of poppy seeds and mustard seeds; brownish-black mustard seeds are not only used as a spice but are crushed to make the oil which gives Bengali cooking its distinctive flavor.

Bengali cuisine is considered elaborate and refined. Bengal is the only place in India where food is served in separate courses, the chronology based on ancient beliefs relating to aiding the digestive process. Bitter leaves and gourd are always served first, followed by rice, *dal*, chutney

and the ubiquitous fish. Even the so-called vegetarians of Bengal, who refuse all meat, eat fish and shrimp. Affluent Bengalis also eat meat on occasion. Mishti Doi (sweetened yogurt set in clay pots) is a Bengali delicacy served at the end of the meal, usually with another milk dessert.

The land of South India is essentially composed of solidified iron-rich lava dating back some 50 million years or more. Rice is known to have been grown in this region as far back as 500 B.C., and an efficient irrigation system developed. The Dravidian culture of the south is considerably older than the Aryan culture which influenced the north. Ancient records in the Tamil script, which pre-dates even Sanskrit, indicate that this was a highly developed and religious land. Architectural wonders depicting Hindu epics and gods mark the entire land south of the Vindhya Mountains, an area where art and music are still preserved and practiced in their traditional forms.

Food, too, retains much of its traditional style in the south and regardless of class, Southern Indians still sit cross-legged on a floor mat to eat from a stainless steel plate (thali) or a piece of fresh banana leaf.

Rice, the southern staple, is everywhere and appears in many different guises: steamed, puffed, made into paper-thin crepes known as dosai or steamed to form idli. Both dosai and idli are made by soaking rice and dal overnight in buttermilk until fermented, then grinding them to make a paste; this is either steamed to make dumplings or idli, or pan-fried to make dosai. These two foods are eaten with different chutneys, vegetables and light dal broths known as Sambar.

In Karnataka, the central southern state, some wheat variations like Mandige exist; this is a delicate dough baked on a heated tile and stuffed with a variety of ingredients including sugar, ground cardamom and shredded coconut. The basic meal consists of vegetables which accompany the universally popular dosai, idli, or steamed rice.

Eggplant is a favorite southern vegetable, seasoned with ghee, salt, fenugreek and dal; roasted in oil; spiced, or

ABOVE LEFT: Offerings of coconut, bananas, flowers and incense on display at a market stall in a typical southern Indian village. ABOVE RIGHT: The Kerala backwaters, fringed by endless coconut groves.

cooked directly over charcoal. The bitter gourd, a popular vegetable not always to Western taste, is salted to remove most of the bitterness. It is then stuffed with a variety of spices and tied with a string before being fried in oil or cooked with an unrefined sugar syrup to offset any bitterness.

Relishes abound and are generally pungent. Balaka is made of red chilies soaked in salt water, dried, then fried in oil to make a crisp and spicy accompaniment. Papads or poppadums, paper-fine disks of wheat or rice-flour and lentil flour, are crisply fried and eaten together with meals.

Sweets in the south are normally variations of rice. Star of the somewhat limited repertoire of desserts is Payasam, consisting of wheat vermicelli, *dal* such as Bengal Gram (*channa dal*), or sometimes sago cooked in sugared milk and spiced with cardamom.

Even though largely vegetarian, the south has its hybrid groups like the Kodavas, who cook rice with chunks of meat, serving it with a spicy sesame chutney. Steamed balls of rice constitute Kadambaputt, which is eaten with pork cooked with the purplish-black kokum fruit, the acidity of which keeps the fat on the meat firm and springy. Popular fish include sardines and a tiny whitebait, crisply fried and eaten whole, bones and all.

The coastal area of Kerala, which has been subjected to foreign influences for thousands of years, is a strong fish and meat-eating region. Jewish settlers came to Kerala as long ago as A.D. 7, bringing with them the notion of slaughtering lifestock as humanely as possible so that the meat was acceptable or kosher (a concept adopted by Muslims, who refer to such food as *halal*).

Syrian Christians escaping persecution at home settled in the southwestern state of Kerala during the 4th century. Not being bound by Hindu prohibitions on beef, Kerala's Christians have developed a number of beef dishes where the meat is tenderized by various means (usually with vinegar or by parboiling before transforming it into a rich coconut milk curry). They are also renowned for their wild duck dishes, where the duck is either cooked to make a curry or stuffed and roasted, the latter being a traditional Christmas dish. Wild boar, cooked with a tangy *masala* or pickled with oil, is another famous Syrian Christian dish.

The Muslims of Kerala love their soups of rice and wheat laced with spices and coconut milk. Kiskiya, a whole wheat porridge cooked with minced meat, is an all time favorite.

Apart from the British, other foreigners who established themselves in India were the Portuguese, who remained in their colony of Goa, north of Kerala, from the 16th century until after Indian independence from the British, finally quitting in 1961. Goans are known for their use of vinegar and kokum fruit (other Indians add sourness with tamarind, lime juice, dried mango powder or, in some areas, kokum) as well as for their love of fiery chilies. Classic examples of Goan cuisine are the pork curry, Vindaloo, which gets its name from the Portuguese words for vinegar and garlic, and Sorpotel, a sour hot curry of pork, liver and pig's blood. Portuguese priests are

thought to have introduced the art of distillation, thus giving birth to the famous Goan *feni*, which is distilled from the fermented sap of the cashew nut and the coconut palm.

Gujarat is the haven of vegetarians. Millet, barley and wheat are equally loved, and snacks are the Gujarati art-form. Nasto is made from chickpea flour, mixed with an assortment of spices and fried. Chevda, or beaten rice, is fried and mixed with salt, spices, almonds, raisins and peanuts.

Zoroastrians came in large numbers to settle in India when they were hounded out of Persia as far back as A.D. 850. Parsis, as they are now known, settled largely in Gujarat. They brought with them a strong meat-eating tradition and a love of egg dishes, raisins, nuts, butter and cream. They inevitably absorbed Gujarati influences and a hybrid cuisine developed. One of the most famous of these dishes is the Parsi fish steamed in banana leaf packets. Another widely known Parsi dish is Dhansak, a one-pot meal combining several types of dal with spices, meat and vegetables.

Islam swept into India as long ago as the 8th century, but it was not until the 16th century that the Muslims gained control over large parts of northern India, converting millions of people to their faith. The Mughul dynasties, which ruled various independent states of pre-Independence India, upstaged the mainstream Hindu culture and cuisine significantly. New flavors, rich relishes, meats with cream and butter sauces, dates, nuts and delectable sweets were the hallmarks of a cuisine that is now widely known and famed for its exotic, non-vegetarian food, rich and aromatic with the memories and music of a far-distant land.

At Home and Abroad

It is undisputed among gourmets that Indian food ranks as one of the world's greatest cuisines. However, like many other fine cuisines, it does not always travel well, either abroad or within its vast homeland. Visitors to India, who normally eat in their hotels, are likely to come away without any idea of the astonishing regional variety of food and the excellence of home cooking, unless they are fortunate enough to have Indian friends invite them into their homes or into some of the interesting regional restaurants.

They will probably also leave convinced that tandoori food is India's most popular, despite the fact that it's virtually impossible to find a clay tandoor oven in an Indian home and that this style of cooking originates in just one region of India, the northwest or Punjab. The current wide-spread popularity of tandoori foods in restaurants is a relatively recent phenomenon and largely attributable to the fact that the Punjabis are among the most mobile of India's ethnic groups and enjoy eating their own food when they go out. Other affluent Indians, who eat their own style of cuisine regularly at home, like to try something

The rich flavor and exotic ingredients introduced by the Mughals make this type of food among the most popular in India.

different when they dine out and find that the tandoori food of the Punjabis is very much to their taste.

"Home cooking" throughout the country is usually simple fare where rice, bread and *dal* constitute the core of the meal. Each region and each household then adds its own distinctive touch with the vegetables, meat, fish and the "ticklers" (pickles, crunchy papads, yogurt-based salads and raita).

Although there are thousands of wonderful Indian recipes, most have been orally handed down from mother to daughter. Wealthy families and the Maharajas patronized a style of cuisine which was unique and where cooks were often employed to create and cook just a single dish in their lifetime. In Lucknow, a *nawab* discovered the technique of slow cooking with steam inside the pot (*dum*), lid sealed, and dough and hot coals placed on top. A chain of hotels introduced this type of cuisine to a broader market within India, after much research in tracking down the often illiterate old cooks. Similarly, much work was done to find and standardize the variety of dishes which come from the Malabar Coast of Southwest India.

There is a slow but growing emergence of small chef-proprietor restaurants throughout India today. The major constraint here is financial, as real estate in major Indian cities like Mumbai and Delhi is prohibitive. What draws people from all backgrounds to these eateries is the freshness and consistency of the food. Unfortunately, these places—such as the seafood restaurants, Gujarati *thali* houses in Bombay and the South Indian fast food outlets or *darshinis* in Bangalore—remain largely inaccessible to the foreign traveler. Some top Indian hotels, however, aware of criticism of the domination of Punjabi-style tandoor cuisine, are now starting to offer menus that reflect the enormous variety of India's culinary heritage on their menus.

ABOVE: Despite an army of servants, *memsahibs* often found entertaining a challenging affair in India.

The Great Spice Bazaar

Walk into an Indian home at mealtime or into a good Indian restaurant and you will be engulfed by a wave of heavenly aromas. Without doubt, the most distinctive feature of Indian food is its creative combination of spices which give an inimitable flavor and aroma. The use of spices in India was recorded in Sanskrit texts 3,000 years ago. The Ayurveda, an ancient treatise on health covering aspects of both mental and physical health, sets out principles for healthy living— including lists of various spices and their medicinal properties. So great was the importance of spices for seasoning as preservatives and as medicine—not just in India but throughout the world—that the search for their source pushed the Europeans into the Age of Exploration in the 15th century.

Given their long familiarity with spices, it is not surprising that Indian cooks use them as skillfully as an artist uses the colors of his palette. "Spices", in a culinary sense, embraces dried seeds, berries, bark, rhizomes, flowers, leaves and chilies. Each spice has its own culinary and medicinal properties. Certain spices are used whole, others always ground into powder; some are superb with meat but overpower more delicate fish and vegetable dishes. Only a few spices (cardamom, saffron and cinnamon) are used for desserts, yet these same spices also appear in meat dishes. It seems little short of miraculous that the Indian cook remembers which spices to use and in what combination (for recipes are almost never written down).

Any combination of spices is referred to as a *masala*. The most widely used—a fragrant combination of dark, pungent spices including cinnamon, cloves, black pepper and cardamom, with the optional addition of nutmeg, mace and saffron in northern regions—is known as *garam masala*. With such tremendous climatic variations in India, certain spices grow only in particular regions. While cardamoms, cloves and peppers are harvested mainly in the south, the regional market places of Rajasthan, Kashmir and Gujarat also grow many spices, with piles of freshly ground red chilies alongside vivid yellow turmeric, which is flanked by mounds of cardamoms and black peppers.

The most colorful stall in the market, the spice merchant, pales in comparison with the fields where turmeric and red chilies are harvested and dried. In the stark yellow deserts of Rajasthan, the spice fields have a colorful splendor quite their own. One of the glorious sights of Kashmir are the fields of purplish-blue crocuses, whose fine thread-like orange stigmas are harvested in October and November.

Although India is modernizing and neat plastic packets of spices can be bought all over the country, many housewives still buy loose spices from the spice merchant and grind their spices just before cooking. But what of "curry powder," that ingredient which some Western cooks consider the basis of all Indian curries? No Indian cook would dream of using the same combination of spices for all types of food. There are specific combinations of whole or ground spices (*masala*) for certain dishes, but these are never used alone. Curry powder as sold outside India was initially developed in Madras for nostalgic British trying to recapture the flavors of India after they returned home.

The medicinal properties of spices are taken into account when food is prepared, as well as the interaction of each spice with the properties of a vegetable or *dal*. Some vegetables and *dals* are supposed to create gas in the body, so asafoetida, cinnamon and cumin are used to balance this. Turmeric is an antiseptic and drunk mixed with hot milk to check internal hemorrhages. Regular use in everyday foods helps prevent internal wounds and infections.

Clove, fennel and cardamom tea has many benefits, especially for the common cold, upset stomach and chill. Saffron boiled in milk is supposed to check anemia and help restore strength. Ginger crushed with honey is sure to cure the worst cough and garlic will not only keep cholesterol levels down, but reduce the ill effects of toxins in the body. Fenugreek seeds roasted in oil help ease arthritic pains, asafoetida roasted on an iron griddle and mixed with salt helps clear gastric disorders. Every Indian home uses spices for natural cures, the recipes passed down for countless generations from the ancient religious texts.

LEFT: Spices have been used for their medicinal properties as well as for flavoring and preservation since time immemorial. ABOVE: Nutmegs being weighed in the wholesale spice market of Cochin.

Indian food abroad is a different matter. Although "curry" has been around in Britain since the days of the Raj, it was, for many years, just a spicy alternative to bland British fare and bore little resemblance to anything produced in Indian homes. During the 1970s, however, genuine interest and awareness of food developed and Indian restaurants became aware of the new upmarket demands for authenticity, freshness and attractive decor. There were Indian cooking programs on television; ingredients like Basmati rice, whole spices, fresh ginger, fresh coriander and curry pastes began to appear on supermarket shelves and eating authentic Indian food became trendy.

This story has been repeated in places as far flung as Hong Kong, Sydney and San Francisco. Indian restaurants in these cities initially catered only to Indians, but as general food awareness increased, so did the number of restaurants where sensitivity in terms of both the food and the decor play an essential role. And with the world-wide trend of "fusion cuisine," where elements of one culinary style are blended with another, one can expect the use of Indian spice blends and Indian vegetables to creep in everywhere. Indian cuisine, despite its ancient traditions, is still evolving and creating new dishes. Travelers look forward to the day when the best of India's regional cuisines will be easily available in the country's better restaurants and hotels. — *Karen Anand*

ABOVE: The ultimate in hospitality in the courtyard of Fort Naila, Rajasthan, owned by The Oberoi Group.

The Honored Guest

The hospitality of Indians, no matter how humble or how lavish their homes, is little short of overwhelming. Part of the explanation for this is that the guest is still seen as an evocation of God and his arrival considered an auspicious event. *Athithya*, a sacred word which means serving a guest, is an important part of a man's social duties and from the Vedic times, guests were ceremoniously received with the traditional yogurt, milk, honey and sugar.

In a land of many poor households, this attitude is still strong, especially in the countryside. Guest is a generic term for anyone who visits and total strangers coming into a village or family are treated with respect; any visitor, even to a poor village, is served water and something sweet. During a festival in some villages in the Punjab, doors are left open to any guest who enters, and they are fed, regardless of class or caste.

Three distinct meal times mark eating patterns everywhere. Breakfast, lunch (which is a far more elaborate meal than Western sandwich lunches) and dinner are uniform. Traditionally, guests would visit only on special occasions and festivals, but in modern India and especially among the middle and upper classes, inviting friends for a meal is now a common social practice. Food is generally served on a banana leaf or a stainless steel *thali*. Washing the hands before meals is an important ritual, since Indians generally use their fingers to eat and the meal is eaten squatting down, usually on the kitchen floor. A small straw mat is placed for sitting and the *thali* or banana leaf is laid in front of the mat, either on the floor or on a low stool.

Families eat together, except for the mother or wife who serves the meal. In middle class homes, however, this role is taken over by the household help. The family normally sits in a straight line and the women of the household serve and refill the *thali* repeatedly. As it is considered discourteous and unclean to serve while eating, the mother or wife serving in a traditional household will not eat until the men have finished. Female guests can either be served with the men or eat with the women later.

Water is sprinkled around the banana leaf or *thali* to purify it before beginning a meal. The *thali* contains all the courses of the meal, but there is usually an order in which the food is eaten. The first mouthfuls of rice are eaten with ghee or chutney and spicy additives. *Dal* is served along with a variety of dry-cooked vegetables seasoned with different spices and garnishes. Papads and relishes are replenished, as are the *dal* and rice. The best portions of fish and meat are always offered to the guest; in Bengal, this would be the head of the fish, regarded as the choicest portion. *Roti* or unleavened bread, *puri* (fried puffed wheat bread) and *paratha* (shallow-fried wheat bread) are common in the north and are eaten with *dal* and vegetables. The sweet, which is milk based, completes the meal,

although in the south it is followed by rice with curds or buttermilk which are believed to soothe the stomach after a spicy meal.

Finally, *paan* or the betel leaf and its seasonings adds that very Indian touch to *athithiya*, apart from acting as a digestive. This leaf is chewed along with a slice of areca nut, a dab of slaked lime and a smear of *katha* paste (another wood extract). Primarily a southern practice, *paan* is now eaten at all times of the day all the way up to the northeast. Artistically crafted *paan* containers or *pandaan* in copper, brass and silver hold the different ingredients. *Paan* concoctions have grown elaborate and up to 15 condiments can be added, including the infamous but popular *zarda*, or chewing tobacco. The *pandaans* are carefully perforated to allow air circulation and come together with a tool designed for slicing the areca nut; these are often exquisitely designed in the shape of celestial figures or adorned with amorous carvings. Spittoons to carry the residue of the saliva and chewed leaf are elaborate vessels of metal. The betel quid can mean many things: hospitality; moral and legal commitment; a digestive; and a fitting end to the remarkable hospitality displayed during a meal.

An alternative digestive to *paan* is the delightful mixture of spices (especially aniseed-flavored fennel), dried fruits (sometimes coated with silver leaf), tiny sugar-coated balls, sugar crystals drenched with rose essence and other tangy combinations known collectively as *supari*. It is so popular that airlines within India offer passengers the choice of boiled sweets or tiny packets of *supari*, continuing the tradition of honoring a guest.

ABOVE: Even Indian gods are believed to be tempted by earthly food.

The Indian Kitchen
A place of sanctity and surprising simplicity

The traditional Indian kitchen was once considered an area of sanctity, with many taboos on who could enter, how they should be dressed and the ways in which pollution could be avoided. Most of this has changed today, although the importance of the Indian hearth within the home is still paramount in most Indian households.

Millions of Indian kitchens are essentially very simple, with the stove set in the center. Although this stove, or *chula*, is often heated by charcoal, in the countryside, dried cow-dung cakes and wood shavings are still widely used. In fact, dried dung is actually considered more "pure" than any other type of fuel and provides a gentle heat ideal for slow cooking. Modern gas stoves have replaced the *chula* in many middle class urban homes.

Cooking ranges and electric gadgets, such as rice cookers and blenders, are slowly appearing in urban Indian homes, but since many of these households can afford kitchen help, traditional methods are preserved for taste and authenticity.

Since the *chula* is normally placed on the floor, most Indian women cook sitting down on a small wooden stool. For this reason, shoes—which might bring in dirt from the outside—are rarely allowed into a traditional Indian kitchen. A large wok-like cooking utensil called the *kadai*, is used for stir-fry-

ing. The *kadai*, which is made of iron, brass or aluminum, is slightly deeper than a **wok**, but the latter makes an excellent substitute.

For cooking rice and curries, a flat-lidded, straight-sided pan known as a *degchi* is used. These were traditionally made of lined brass, but are now generally made of aluminum and very inexpensive, even if less attractive.

Almost any **saucepan** can be used for cooking Indian dishes, but take care to choose one that has a non-reactive lining, since many Indian dishes contain acid. **Nonstick skillets** are ideal for Indian cooking as they avoid the problem of spices sticking to the bottom of the skillet. It is also perfect for those who are more health-conscious, as it allows the use of less oil when frying.

Indian breads are rolled out with a wooden rolling pin on a flat circular stone slab or wooden board and cooked on a heavy iron griddle, or *tawa*. A **heavy cast iron skillet** or **pancake griddle** makes a good substitute.

Spices and various seasonings such as ginger, garlic and onions, as well as grains such as rice and lentils are ground at home. The grinding stone is such an important symbol of the hearth and home that in some areas of the country, the bride stands on a grinding stone during part of the wedding ceremony, symbolizing that she is now mistress of her own household.

Small amounts of spices are crushed just before cooking, either on a flat granite slab or, in the south, in a black stone concave bowl. Large slabs of granite with a granite rolling pin are used for grinding large amounts of seasonings or grain. Modern cooks can use a **mortar and pestle** or will find a **blender, food processor or spice grinder** a welcome substitute for the grinding stone; ideal for grinding spices quickly and effortlessly.

Steaming utensils for making *idli* in the south and *farsan* in Gujarat are common, some of them are now made to fit into pressure cookers. Other regional cuisines demand special utensils, such as the cylindrical clay ovens, or tandoor, used to bake Mughul-style breads and meats in the north. In Kashmir, samovars bubble all day long, brewing the favorite aromatic green tea, *kahwah*, together with green cardamoms and almonds.

Coconut graters are essential items in Bengali and southern Indian kitchens. A serrated iron disk mounted on wood, and often hand-cranked, is used for removing the fibers from the coconut as well as for shredding and grating the flesh.

OPPOSITE: Most spices are bought whole and freshly ground at home. LEFT: A lined copper *kadai* for stir-frying. ABOVE: An old fuel stove with a griddle or *tawa* for cooking flatbreads. BELOW: A traditional granite grinding slab.

Split bamboo baskets are used for straining the coconut milk and also serve as multi-purpose sieves. They are particularly attractive in the northeast, where they are intricately woven and come in all sizes.

In meat-eating homes of the north and south, solid wooden chopping blocks and cleavers are used. An all-purpose **meat cleaver** and **thick wooden board** are useful additions to any kitchen where Indian food is to be prepared. **Soup ladles**, generally of steel or aluminum with rounded ends, are used for stirring *dal* and curries, while **small wire mesh baskets with long wooden handles** are used to retrieve items after deep-frying. Simple but attractive unglazed earthenware bowls are used for setting yogurt; any glass or ceramic bowl or jar can be used instead.

Eating utensils are uniform across India, with the stainless steel *thali* or tray set with a variety of small bowls for curries, *dal* and yogurt. The old *thalis* were made of brass, bell metal or silver, but stainless steel is preferred today because it is cheap and easy to clean. Porcelain and melamine tableware have invaded middle class homes everywhere, yet the stainless steel *thali* is still the most common eating plate. Many Indians prefer to eat with their right hand, believing that the food actually tastes better or that cutlery is unhygienic. Despite this, many middle class families use a spoon and fork at mealtimes.

In the southern and eastern areas of India, one versatile utensil is invariably found during festivals and weddings: a square of freshly picked banana leaf, which makes the perfect, biodegradable disposable plate.

A Few Simple Cooking Methods

Although Indian cuisine involves using an often complex blending of spices and sometimes two or three different cooking methods during the preparation of a single dish, it is very much easier than it sounds.

Most Indian dishes involve the use of spices, which ideally should be roasted and ground fresh when preparing any dish. As each spice takes a different amount of time to release its flavor and aroma, it is important to follow the correct order given when dry-roasting spices in a skillet. To be sure of maximum flavor and aroma, always try to buy whole spices and grind them just before cooking. First, roast the spices gently in a dry skillet over low heat, stirring continuously until they start to smell fragrant. Take care that they do not burn. Cool slightly, then grind in a small blender or food processor.

Ground spices are then usually gently stir-fried in oil or ghee, either alone or together with meat or vegetables. Be sure to keep the temperature low and to continuously stir the ground spices so they do not stick to the bottom of the skillet. Using plenty of oil or ghee helps ensure the spices do not stick; if you're health conscious, you might like to pour off any excess oil once the ground spices are cooked, or use a nonstick skillet.

Many vegetable dishes and curries are, after the initial *bhuna* or stir-frying stage, simmered over very low heat on the top of the stove. The skillet is often kept covered to ensure that the aromas do not escape. An exception to this is when coconut milk is used, particularly in southern Indian dishes. As coconut milk tends to curdle or break apart easily, it should always be brought to a boil slowly, stirring frequently and lifting up the milk with a large ladle and pouring it back down into the pan. Once it has come to a boil, it should always be simmered uncovered.

Additional seasoning is often added just before the food is served to intensify the flavor. This may be as simple as a sprinkle of aromatic sweet *garam masala*, or, especially in southern India, the addition of some fried brown mustard seeds, dried chilies and curry leaves. Interestingly, this stage is known as "tempering," after the Portuguese *temperado*, meaning "to season".

Before it is used in Indian dishes, yogurt is often vigorously stirred to ensure that the whey or liquid is properly incorporated with the curds; this is referred to as whipped yogurt. Yogurt is also frequently hung to drain off some of the whey and obtain thicker curds before adding to the other ingredients. Although this is done using cheese cloth or muslin fabric in India, cooks elsewhere may find an easier method is to place the yogurt in a paper-lined coffee filter and set the cone-shaped device over a jar. The whey will drip through, leaving the curds in the filter. This is hung yogurt, which is preferred as the texture remains unchanged during cooking.

RIGHT: The ultimate in Indian dining, an elegantly laid antique table set with *thalis* of Rajasthani food, while attentive retainers hover nearby.
ABOVE: Free communal meals are served to literally thousands of guests at religious festivals.

Authentic Indian Ingredients

Asafoetida is a strong-smelling brown resin. Known in India as *hing*, it adds an onion flavor to cooked food and is believed to aid digestion. Often used in lentil dishes, it is sold in a box or tin as a solid lump, or in the form of powder.

Banana leaves can be purchased frozen or fresh from Asian food stores in many parts of the world. As well as being used as a plate to serve meals on, banana leaves are also used to wrap food in while cooking; the leaves infuse a delicate flavor and aroma to the food. Before using to wrap food, the leaves need to be softened in boiling water to avoid cracking.

Basmati rice is an Indian long-grain rice characterized by its thinness and fragrance. The grains stay whole and separate when cooked with oil and spices. Substitute with long-grain, Thai jasmine rice.

Besan flour is a pale yellow flour which has been finely ground from *channa dal* (Bengal gram) or the yellow split pea. It is sometimes referred to as chickpea flour, Bengal gram flour or simply gram flour. It is commonly found in Asian food stores and some health food stores.

Cardamom is an aromatic spice pod native to India. The more common

cardamom pods are small, green or straw-colored, and contain a dozen or so tiny, intensely aromatic black seeds. Large black cardamom pods, which are at least six times the size of the green cardamoms, are used mainly in savory dishes. Do not buy ground cardamom as it is virtually flavorless compared with the heavenly fragrance of the freshly roasted and ground whole spice. Bruise the pods lightly if using the spice whole.

Carom seeds are derived from the same family as cumin and parsley, and are known as bishop's weed in the West, and *ajwain* in India. The seeds are similar in appearance and flavor to caraway seeds, but with strong overtones of thyme. Look for the seeds in Indian specialty stores; it is worth trying to locate this spice as its use makes a subtle difference to the final flavor of many dishes. If unavailable, substitute with dried thyme.

Cashews are used in northern Indian cooking to provide substance as well as a nutty fragrance to curry gravies. Indian recipes that call for cashews require fresh, unsalted and unroasted cashew nuts.

Chickpeas are also known as garbanzo beans and are light tan in color and pea-shaped in appearance, with a firm texture and a nutty flavor. Look for dried or canned chickpeas in well stocked supermarkets and health food stores.

Chili is used both fresh and dried in Indian cooking. Dried red chilies have a very different flavor from fresh red or green chilies. Dried chilies should be cut or broken into pieces and soaked in hot water for about 10 minutes to soften before grinding. In Goan recipes, the chilies are normally soaked in vinegar rather than water. If you want to reduce the heat without losing the flavor, slit open the chilies and discard some or all of the seeds before preparing.

Chili paste is made by simply grinding fresh chilies to a paste in a blender or food processor. Jars of chili paste are available in many Asian food stores, but many other ingredients are often added, such as sugar, garlic, salt and vinegar, so check the label and taste before using. Make your own fresh chili paste whenever possible, and remove the seeds before grinding if you prefer a milder flavor.

Chironji nuts are small brownish nuts which look a little like large sunflower seeds. They are sometimes ground together with other nuts, such as cashews or almonds, or with white poppy seeds to enrich the sauces of some dishes. The flavor is similar to that of hazelnuts, although they are perhaps best substituted with a mixture of hazelnuts and almonds.

Cinnamon is lighter in color, thinner, and more expensive than cassia bark, which is often sold as cinnamon. Cassia bark has a stronger flavor than cinnamon, but makes an acceptable substitute. Do not use ground cinnamon as a substitute where cinnamon sticks are called for.

Cloves are native to the Moluccan islands of Indonesia, though they have been grown in India for centuries. Use the whole, dark brown nail-shaped spice rather than ground cloves. Store in an airtight container away from light.

Coconut cream and **coconut milk** are used frequently in Indian cooking. While freshly pressed milk has more flavor, coconut cream and milk are now widely sold in cans and packets that are quick, convenient and tasty. You should add 1 cup of water to 1 cup of canned or packet coconut cream to obtain **thick coconut milk**, and 2 cups of water to 1 cup of coconut cream to obtain **thin coconut milk**. If you prefer to use fresh coconuts, you will first need to open the coconut by tapping firmly on the center with the blunt end of a cleaver until a crack appears. Drain the juice and continue tapping until the coconut cracks into two. Place the coconut halves in a moderate oven for 15 to 20 minutes until the flesh shrinks away from the shell. Remove the meat from the shell, use a vegetable peeler to remove the outer brown skin, then grate the flesh using a blender or food processor. If you end up with more than you need, freshly grated coconut keeps well in the freezer. Fresh Coconut cream is made by grating the flesh of 1 coconut, adding $1/2$ cup water, kneading a few times, then straining with your fist, or with a muslin or cheesecloth. This should

yield about $1/2$ cup of coconut cream. Thick coconut milk is obtained by the same method, but the water is doubled to 1 cup and it should yield about 1 cup of thick coconut milk. Thin coconut milk is obtained by adding 1 cup of water to the already pressed coconut flesh a second time and straining again, this should yield 1 cup of thin coconut milk.

Coconut vinegar is made from the sap of the coconut palm and is sold in bottles. It is low in acidity and has a musty flavor. It is often used in dishes that require a piquant flavor. The vinegar is frequently used in Filipino as well as southern Indian cooking. If this cannot be found, substitute with rice vinegar or cider vinegar, diluted 1 part water to 4 parts vinegar.

Coriander leaves, also known as cilantro or Chinese parsely, are used as a herb and garnish in Indian cooking. Fresh coriander leaves should keep for 5 to 6 days if you wash and dry the leaves thoroughly before placing them in a plastic bag. Dried **coriander seeds** are round and beige, and are perhaps the most widely used spice in India. When ground they release a warm, nutty, slightly citrus-like aroma. Whole coriander seeds have a stronger flavor than ground dried coriander powder, which quickly loses its aroma.

Cumin (*jeera*) is used either whole or the seeds are roasted and then ground to a fine powder. Cumin seeds range in color from the more common pale

brown (above left), to a light green and black (above right). Cumin seeds are believed to aid digestion and are used in most Indian spice blends.

Curry leaves are an important herb in southern Indian cooking. The small, dark green leaf has a distinctive flavor which is sadly missing from the dried herb. When a sprig of curry leaves is called for in a recipe, this usually means 8–12 individual leaves.

Dal is often spelled as "dhal" in English; this term covers a variety of dried lentils. The major ones are: **Bengal gram** (*channa dal*), which resembles a small yellow pea and is often sold split and used as a seasoning (substitute with yellow split peas); *moong dal*, the small green mung bean that is sprouted to make bean sprouts; **Black gram dal** (*urad dal*), which is sold either with its black skin still on (substitute with black lentils) or when husked, is creamy white in color (substitute with white lentils); *masoor dal*, salmon-pink lentils; *toor*, *tuvar* or *arhar dal*, a pale yellow lentil which is smaller than the Bengal gram; and *kabuli channa* or chickpeas, which is known by their Spanish name, *garbanzos*, in some Western countries. The various types of *dal* can usually be found in Indian specialty stores, supermarkets and health food stores.

Dried mango powder (*amchoor*) is used to give a sour tang to Indian dishes. It is ground from dried unripe green mangoes. If it is not available, a squeeze of lemon juice makes an acceptable substitute.

Fennel is similar in appearance to cumin although slightly longer and fatter. Fennel has a sweet fragrance that is similar to aniseed. Some Indian cooks wrongly translate *saunf*, the word for fennel, as aniseed, but the latter spice is not found in India. The seeds are used whole or ground.

Fenugreek is an almost square, hard, yellowish-brown seed. The seeds are strongly flavored and are often used in southern Indian dishes and in pickles.

Garam masala is a blend of several strongly aromatic spices such as coriander, cumin, peppercorns and cardamom, designed to add flavor and fragrance to meat dishes. Pre-blended *garam masala* can be bought from any store specializing in spices, but the flavor is incomparable to freshly ground *garam masala* made at home (page 23). Store the ground powder in an airtight jar away from heat or sunlight.

Ghee is clarified butter with the milk solids removed. Widely used in Indian cooking, it can be heated to high temperatures without burning and adds a rich and delicious flavor to food. While ghee can be found in many Asian food stores, it may be substituted with butter or vegetable oil.

Limes of various types are used in Indian cuisine. Large limes have a tart flavor similar to lemons. Small green limes, frequently known as *calamansi*, are about the size of a walnut and have a less acidic, more fragrant juice. These are preferred when used to squeeze over dishes before serving.

Mace is the lacy orange-red covering,

or aril, of the nutmeg seed. It is often sold in the form of dried blades and is also avaible in a powdered form.

Mangoes are a popular tropical fruit, that vary in size, shape and color—ripe mangoes range from green to yellow to red. Unripe and ripe green mangoes are used in Indian cooking. Unripe green mangoes are very sour, have a firmer flesh and are often used in pickles or chutneys.

Mustard oil is vegetable oil infused with ground mustards seeds and used for cooking as well as preserving. It is particularly popular in Bengal. The flavor is distinct and is worth looking for in Indian specialty stores; if mustard oil is not available, substitute any refined vegetable oil.

Mustard Seeds are either brownish-black (above left) or yellow (above right). Brown-black mustard seeds are more common in southern Indian cuisine as they impart a nutty flavor to dishes. Try to use the type specified.

Nigella seeds are often incorrectly referred to as onion seeds. These small black seeds are known as

kalonji in India. Omit if not available; or when call for in Indian breads, substitute with black sesame seeds.

Nutmeg, like cloves, is a spice native to the Moluccan islands of Indonesia. The nutmeg is actually the seed of a fleshy fruit, and is covered by a lacy red membrane known as mace. Store whole nutmegs in a glass jar. Whole nutmeg should always be freshly grated before using.

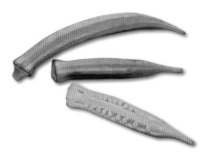

Okra is also known as ladies' fingers and is a variety of banana. It is a green, curved, ridged vegetable, ranging from $2^1/_2$ to 8 inches (7 to 20 cm) in length. Okra has long been popular in India and Southeast Asia as a vegetable.

Palm sugar is made from the sap of coconut palms or the arenga sugar palm tree. Palm sugar varies in color from gold to dark brown. It is less sweet than cane sugar and has a distinct, rich flavor. Dark brown sugar, maple syrup or a mixture of sugar and molasses are good substitutes.

Paneer is a kind of Indian curd cheese which is made by mixing milk with vinegar to form a curd, then draining the curd through a muslin cloth and leaving to set for a few hours under the weight of a heavy object (see page 27 for Homemade Paneer recipe). Vegetarians may prefer to substitute firm tofu in the recipes that call for paneer, and cream cheese or ricotta may also be substituted.

Peppercorns are dried green berries, borne from a vine thought to be native to the Malabar Coast of India. The dried peppercorns are generally sold black (that is, with their skin intact) and are used both whole, or when black pepper is called for, freshly ground.

Poppadums, are wafer-thin disks of seasoned wheat and lentil flour which swell up and become deliciously crisp after deep-frying in hot oil. Make sure they are thoroughly dry before frying. If you live in a humid climate, it is worth drying them in the oven on low heat for 30 minutes before frying as that will make them more crispy. Serve as an accompaniment to Indian meals and store unused poppadums in an airtight container in a cool and dry place as they can grow moldy under humid conditions.

Poppy seeds are tiny, white seeds prized for their delicate nutty flavor. Used as a thickening agent, they are generally soaked in warm water for 10–15 minutes, then ground. Substitute with cashew nuts or almonds.

Saffron is the world's most expensive

spice. The dried strands should be allowed to infuse in warm milk before being added to rice and dessert dishes. Store saffron in the freezer as it loses its fragrance quickly, and never buy powdered saffron if you want the true aroma of this spice.

Shallots (*hormlek*) are small and round and have a pinkish-purple color. Shallots add a sweet oniony flavor and a hint of garlic to countless dishes. They are also sliced, deep-fried and used as a garnish.

Star anise is a dried pod with an average of eight hard brown petals. The star-shaped pods encase shiny black seeds which have a marked aniseed flavor. Coastal Indian communities with a long history of trade with the Far East use this Chinese spice in their dishes. The whole spice is usually used. Whole star anise that is stored in an airtight container will keep for at least a year.

Tamarind is the sour fruit of a very large, tropical evergreen tree, and its juice is used as a souring agent in

many Indian dishes, particularly in southern India. More commonly available as a dried pulp and sold in plastic packets, bottled concentrated tamarind juice is also available. If using the dried pulp, soak the dried pulp in warm water to soften, then mash well and strain to remove any seeds or fibers. The strained juice is what is used. The dried pulp is sometimes used directly without this preliminary soaking; be sure to pick it over carefully first and discard any fibers and stones. Make sure you purchase the naturally sour tamarind pulp and not the sweetened variety. Stored in an airtight container, the pulp keeps almost indefinitely.

Turmeric is a member of the ginger family. Turmeric is always dried in India and sold as a dried root or in powdered form. Purchase turmeric as you need it as the flavor can fade over time. As this bright yellow spice is very frequently adulterated with rice flour, you may find that the amounts specified in the recipes seem insufficient. Adjust according to taste but be aware that turmeric is quite pungent. Be careful, as it can also stain clothing and plastic utensils.

Yogurt is often vigorously stirred (use a hand-held mixer) to ensure the liquid whey is reincorporated with the curds; this is referred to as **whipped yogurt**. Some Indian dishes call for a solid yogurt called **hung yogurt**. The thicker curd is desired for its firm texture. You can obtain this by simply pouring off the liquid whey if it has already separated, or by placing it in a muslin cloth or paper-lined coffee filter and setting it over a jar or hanging it over the kitchen sink. The whey, or liquid, will drip out and leave behind the yogurt solids.

Authentic Indian Recipes

Planning an Indian meal

Appetizers like Samosa, Pakora and crisp Poppadum wafers, which can be purchased dried and freshly deep-fried, are wonderful starters or accompaniments. The courses that follow normally include a fish, meat or poultry curry, vegetable dishes, accompaniments such as pickles and chutneys (try Lemon Mango Pickles or Tamarind Ginger Chutney) and a bowl of yogurt or Raita. Yogurt has a wonderful cooling effect on the palate, especially when mixed with rice. Combine one or two spicy gravy or curry dishes with dishes that are dry or grilled and not as spicy. Serve main courses with rice and Indian breads like Tandoori Naan or Paratha—which can be torn apart and used to scoop up sauces. Instead of plain rice, try a fragrant Coconut or Lemon Rice. There are endless combinations. As a general guide, the recipes in this book will serve 4–6 people as part of a meal containing an appetizer and three to four main dishes served with rice or Indian bread.

Indian spices

The secret to authentic Indian cooking is the unique blend of fragrant spices that is used to prepare each dish. While many of the same spices are used over and over—cumin, coriander, turmeric, fenugreek, fennel, cardamom, ginger, garlic—by subtly varying the blend, each dish obtains a distinct flavor and aroma. There is no such thing as a "curry powder" in India—this was a colonial invention for the export market—but any complex combination of spices is referred to as a *masala*. Once you purchase the individual spices it is both fun and easy to prepare and experiment with your own blends at home. Most whole and ground spices will keep for several months. Whole dried spices are generally dry-roasted in a skillet or fried in a small quantity of oil before being ground to a paste in a blender or spice grinder. The heating process "unlocks" the aromas in the dried spices and makes the flavors come alive. In many parts of Asia, freshly ground spice pastes are also available and these are wonderful if you can find them. But try to avoid dried prepared "curry powders" as these do not recreate the same complexity of flavors needed for most Indian dishes. Store any leftover powder or paste in a jar, or in plastic wrap, inside the freezer.

Ingredients

The recipes that follow list all the ingredients you will need to create an authentic Indian dish. The final result is worth the effort of locating the ingredients listed and in most cases they are available in Asian food stores or markets. A list of mail-order/online sources is also given on page 112.

Time estimates

Estimates are given for preparation and cooking, and are based on the assumption that a spice grinder, food processor or blender will be used.

Tips on grinding spices

Spice grinding attachments for blenders and food processors are easily available and inexpensive these days. Pulse the grinder to allow the spices to settle and grind evenly and allow roasted spices to cool before grinding. Slice larger ingredients first, grind tougher ingredients before the softer ones, and avoid overloading by grinding in batches. Either add a little liquid to keep the blades turning, or remove the spice attachment and shake gently to loosen the spices.

Spice Mixtures

Garam Masala

$1/_2$ cup (75 g) cumin seeds
2 tablespoons coriander seeds
3 cinnamon sticks (3 in/8 cm each)
10–12 green cardamom pods, bruised
4–5 black cardamom pods, bruised
10 cloves
$1/_2$ nutmeg, broken
3–4 blades mace
1 tablespoon black peppercorns
4 whole star anise
5 bay leaves

1 Dry-roast all the spices in a non-stick wok or skillet and heat over a very low fire, stirring the spices continuously for 2 to 3 minutes until fragrant. Allow to cool, then grind to a powder in a blender or a mortar and pestle. Store in an airtight bottle (if stored in the freezer, spices keep fresh almost indefinitely).

Note: *Garam masala* is called for in many Indian recipes. While the freshly prepared spice mixture is more flavorful, pre-blended *garam masala* can also be found in Asian food stores.

Preparation Time: 10 mins   Cooking Time: 10 mins   Yields $2/_3$ cup

Chaat Masala

1 tablespoon cumin seeds
1 tablespoon black peppercorns
5 cloves
$1/_2$ tablespoon dried mint leaves
$1/_4$ teaspoon carom seeds (*ajwain*)
$1/_4$ teaspoon asafoetida powder
1 tablespoon rock salt
$2^1/_2$ tablespoons dried mango powder (*amchoor*)
1 teaspoon ground ginger
1 teaspoon ground red pepper

$^1/_4$ teaspoon cream of tartar
2 teaspoons salt

1 Dry-roast the first seven ingredients in a nonstick wok or skillet and heat gently, continuously stirring for 2 to 3 minutes until the spices are fragrant. **2** Remove from the heat, add the salt and grind to a powder in a blender or mortar and pestle while still warm. Mix in the remaining ingredients and allow to cool. Store tightly bottled. This salty, sour Chaat Masala (the approximate translation of the name is "finger licking"!) is sprinkled over cooked food for additional flavor.

Preparation Time: 10 mins   Cooking Time: 10 mins   Yields $^1/_2$ cup

Pickles and Chutneys

Mixed Vegetable Pickles
Sabzi Achar

1 medium carrot
2 medium unripe green mangoes (8 oz/250 g)
1 section lotus root (4 oz/125 g)
3–5 green chilies

1 cup (250 ml) mustard oil or vegetable oil
2 teaspoons fennel seeds
1 teaspoon nigella seeds (*kalonji*)
1 teaspoon black mustard seeds
2 teaspoons ground red pepper
2 teaspoons ground turmeric
2 teaspoons Garam Masala (page 23)
1 onion, sliced, then puréed in a blender
1 tablespoon grated ginger
5 cloves garlic, crushed
1 large lemon, deseeded and cut into wedges
3 tablespoons freshly squeezed lime juice
1$^1/_2$ tablespoons salt

1 Peel and cut the carrot and mango into small strips. Peel and slice the lotus root. Leave the chilies whole. **2** Heat the mustard oil in a wok or skillet to smoking point, then add the fennel, nigella and mustard seeds and stir-fry for 1 minute until the spices crackle. Add the red pepper, turmeric, Garam Masala, onion, ginger and garlic, and continue stirring for 3 to 4 minutes. Add the vegetables and lemon wedges. **3** Remove from the heat and add the lime juice and salt. Stir to mix well. Place the mixture in sterilized jars, covering it completely with a layer of mustard oil in order to preserve the pickles. If necessary, add more oil which has first been heated to smoking point, then cooled. Keeps 3 to 4 months.

Preparation Time: 20 mins
Cooking Time: 10 mins

Onion Mustard Pickles
Pyaz Ka Achar

$^1/_2$ cup (125 ml) mustard oil or vegetable oil
2 tablespoons black mustard seeds
1 teaspoon ground red pepper
$^1/_2$ teaspoon ground turmeric
1$^1/_2$ tablespoons white vinegar
2 tablespoons sugar
$^1/_4$ tablespoon salt
1$^1/_2$ tablespoons dried mango powder (*amchoor*)
5–8 green chilies
15 cloves garlic, peeled
1 tablespoon grated ginger
1 tablespoon crushed garlic
1 lb (500 g) onions, peeled and sliced
$^2/_3$ cup (150 ml) of freshly squeezed lime juice

1 Heat the oil in a wok to smoking point, then set aside to cool. **2** Place the mustard seeds, red pepper, turmeric, vinegar, sugar, salt and mango powder in a blender or food processor, and grind to a paste. Add this to the oil, together with the remaining ingredients. **3** Stir to mix well and store in sterilized jars, covering the pickles completely with oil. Keeps 3 to 4 weeks.

Preparation Time: 30 mins   Cooking Time: 3 mins   Yields 4 cups

Lemon Mango Pickles
Nimbu Aur Aam Ka Achar

1 lb (500 g) lemons, washed, cut into wedges and deseeded
5–7 green chilies, halved lengthwise
2 unripe green mangoes (8 oz/250 g), peeled and diced
$^1/_2$ cup (125 ml) lemon juice
1 tablespoon ground cumin
1 tablespoon ground turmeric
1 teaspoon ground red pepper
1$^1/_2$ tablespoons salt
2 tablespoons sugar
1 cup (250 ml) mustard oil or vegetable oil

1 Combine the lemons, chilies, mango and lemon juice in a bowl and sprinkle with the spices, salt and sugar. Place in a large glass jar, cover loosely with a cloth and leave in the sun for 6 days.

2 Heat the oil to smoking point, allow to cool, then stir into the lemon mixture. Leave in the sun for another 4 days then cover the jar with a lid, Store in a cool, dry place away from the light. Keeps for several months.

Preparation Time: 25 mins   Cooking Time: 5 mins   Yields 4 cups

Goan Shrimp Pickles
Mole de Camarao

1/2 cup (125 ml) oil
1 lb (500 g) medium shrimp, peeled and patted dry
1/2 teaspoon cumin seeds
1/4 teaspoon black peppercorns
1 teaspoon ground turmeric
1 medium onion, diced
2–3 cloves garlic
1 tablespoon minced ginger
4 green cardamom pods, seeds removed and husks discarded
10 dried chilies, dry-roasted in a skillet until crisp
1 teaspoon cinnamon
1–2 cups (250–500 ml) white vinegar
1 teaspoon salt

1 Heat the oil in a wok or skillet and stir-fry the shrimp for 5 minutes. Drain and set aside.
2 Grind or blend all the seasonings in a blender or food processor with 2–3 tablespoons of vinegar, to make a paste. Transfer to a saucepan and dilute to a thin sauce with the rest of the vinegar. Simmer over low heat for 30 minutes. Add the salt, then cool.
3 Pack the shrimp into a sterilized glass jar and pour the sauce over the shrimp. Make sure there is a layer of oil covering the top of the shrimp. Allow to pickle for 3 days before eating. This pickle is an ideal accompaniment to any seafood dish and can be kept in the fridge for 1 to 2 months.

Preparation Time: 35 mins
Cooking Time: 40 mins

Tamarind Ginger Chutney
Saunth Ki Chatni

3/4 cup (200 g) tamarind pulp
3 cups (750 ml) hot water
10 dates, stones removed (optional)
2 teaspoons ground red pepper
2 tablespoons grated ginger
1/2 teaspoon nigella seeds (kalonji)
1/2 teaspoon fennel seeds
2 teaspoons cumin seeds
1 cup (120 g) shaved palm sugar or dark brown sugar
2 teaspoons sugar, or more to taste
1/2 teaspoon salt, or more to taste

1 Place the tamarind pulp and hot water in a saucepan. Mash and strain the pulp to obtain the liquid. Add the dates, if using, and simmer over low heat for 30 minutes. Strain to remove the seeds and fiber.
2 Dry-roast the nigella, fennel and cumin seeds in a nonstick wok or skillet for 1 to 2 minutes, stirring continuously until fragrant. Grind the seeds to a powder in a blender or mortar and pestle.
3 Return the strained juice to the saucepan and add the red pepper, ginger and the ground spices. Cook over low heat for 10 minutes, then add the palm sugar and stir until dissolved. Add the sugar and salt and mix thoroughly. Serve with appetizers such as Pakora (page 28) or Vegetable Samosas (page 28), or simple vegetable dishes for extra tang. Will keep in a refrigerator for about 1 week.

Preparation Time: 30 mins   Cooking Time: 40 mins   Yields 1 1/2 cups

Tomato Chutney
Hussaini Tamatar Qoot

2 tablespoons oil
1 1/2 teaspoons black mustard seeds
1 teaspoon nigella seeds (kalonji)
10 curry leaves
2 pinches of asafoetida powder
2 teaspoons crushed garlic
1 1/2 teaspoons grated ginger
3–4 green chilies, slit lengthwise and deseeded

1 can (16 oz/450 g) peeled, whole tomatoes, drained; or 4 medium tomatoes (16 oz/450 g), blanched and peeled
1 teaspoon ground turmeric
2 teaspoons ground red pepper
4 teaspoons sugar
1/2 teaspoon salt

1 Heat the oil in a wok or skillet and fry the mustard and nigella seeds, curry leaves and asafoetida for 1 minute until the spices crackle.
2 Add the garlic and ginger, stir-fry gently for a few minutes, then add the chilies and tomatoes and cook for about 10 minutes until the tomatoes turn pulpy.
3 Add the turmeric, red pepper and sugar and stir until the sugar dissolves. Add the salt and serve hot. This chutney keeps for 3 to 4 days refrigerated, if stored in a covered jar.

Preparation Time: 20 mins   Cooking Time: 15 mins   Yields 1 1/2 cups

Fresh Coconut Chutney
Thenga Chatni

3 cups (250 g) freshly grated coconut
3 green chilies, minced
4–5 cloves garlic, minced
1/2 tablespoon minced ginger
3 tablespoons Bengal gram (channa dal) or yellow split peas
1/2 teaspoon salt

Seasonings
1 teaspoon oil
1/4 teaspoon black mustard seeds
1/2 teaspoon white lentils (urad dal)
1–2 dried chilies, broken and deseeded
5 curry leaves
Pinch of asafoetida powder

1 Prepare the Seasonings by heating the oil in a wok or skillet and stir-frying the ingredients, except for the asafoetida, for 1 minute until the mustard seeds begin to pop. Add the asafoetida, stir, then remove from the heat and set aside.
2 Using a blender or food processor, coarsely grind the coconut with the chilies, garlic, ginger, Bengal gram,

salt, and the mint and coriander leaves if you are making Green Coconut Chutney (recipe below).

3 Add the coconut mixture to the Seasonings and mix well. Serve in a bowl with Dosai (page 40), *idli*, *vadai* or other southern Indian breads and snacks.

Preparation Time: 20 mins   Cooking Time: 5 mins   Yields 1$^3/_4$ cups

Green Coconut Chutney

2 cups (50 g) mint leaves
$^1/_2$ cup (25 g) coriander leaves
  (cilantro)
Ingredients for the Fresh Coconut
  Chutney recipe (recipe above)

1 Follow the recipe for the Fresh Coconut Chutney recipe, adding the mint and coriander leaves when coarsely grinding the coconut mixture in Step 2. Serve with Indian breads and snacks.

Preparation Time: 10 mins
Yields 2 cups

Green Mango Chutney
Mangga Thuvial

3 large unripe green mangoes (total
  of about 1 lb/500 g)
$^1/_2$ teaspoon sesame seeds
3–4 dried chilies, cut into lengths
2 medium onions, diced
2 tablespoons freshly grated or
  moistened unsweetened desiccated
  coconut
10 curry leaves
1 tablespoon minced coriander
  leaves (cilantro)
1 teaspoon oil
1 teaspoon black mustard seeds
$^1/_2$ teaspoon Bengal gram (*channa
  dal*) or yellow split peas
$^1/_4$ teaspoon salt

1 Peel the mangoes, discard the seeds and dice the flesh.
2 Dry-roast the sesame seeds and chilies in a nonstick wok or skillet for 2 minutes until crisp.
3 Place the mango, sesame seeds,

chilies, onion, coconut, curry leaves and coriander leaves in a blender or food processor, and pulse a few times to just mix.
4 Heat the oil in a wok or skillet and stir-fry the mustard seeds and Bengal gram for 1 minute until the mustard seeds begin to pop. Add the mango mixture to the wok and mix well. Season with salt and serve.

Preparation Time: 20 mins   Cooking Time: 5 mins   Yields 4 cups

Mint Coriander Chutney
Pudina Ki Chatni

1 cup (50 g) coriander leaves
  (cilantro)
$^1/_2$ cup (25 g) mint leaves
2 green chilies, sliced
$^1/_2$ in (1 cm) ginger
3 cloves garlic
2 tablespoons yogurt
1 teaspoon sugar
$^1/_2$ teaspoon ground red pepper
$^1/_2$ teaspoon salt
1 teaspoon Chaat Masala (page 23)
$^1/_2$ teaspoon lemon juice

1 Place all the ingredients in a blender and process until smooth. Serve with snacks or tandoori dishes like Tandoori Baked Cauliflower and Stuffed Bell Peppers (page 60).

Preparation Time: 15 mins
Yields $^2/_3$ cup

Sweet Mango Chutney

1 lb (500 g) ripe mangoes, peeled
  and diced
2 tablespoons grated ginger
1 cup (250 g) sugar
2 teaspoons salt
1$^1/_2$ teaspoons ground red pepper
1 teaspoon Garam Masala (page 23)
5 tablespoons freshly squeezed
  lime juice

1 Place the mango and ginger into a saucepan and cook for 8 to 10 minutes over low heat until most of the juice has evaporated.
2 Add the sugar, salt, red pepper, Garam Masala and lime juice, and cook over low heat until the sugar dissolves and the chutney thickens.
3 Cool thoroughly before storing in clean sterilized jars. The chutney may be eaten the next day, but is best served a week later. It can be stored in the refrigerator for up to 3 months. Serve with any Indian meal.

Preparation Time: 15 mins
Cooking Time: 25 mins

Drinks

Festive Nut Spice Milk
Thandai

4 cups (1 liter) fresh milk
3 tablespoons unsalted melon seeds
2 tablespoons blanched almonds
2 tablespoons raw cashew nuts
1$^1/_2$ tablespoons white poppy
  seeds, soaked and simmered in $^1/_2$
  cup (125 ml) water for 15 minutes
1 teaspoon black peppercorns
1 teaspoon fennel seeds
Large pinch of saffron threads
5 green cardamom pods, bruised
Petals from 1 red rose, or a few
  drops of rose essence
1–2 tablespoons sugar
1 heaped tablespoon shelled,
  unsalted pistachio nuts, skins
  removed and finely ground
  (optional)

1 Combine 1 cup (250 ml) of the milk with the rest of the ingredients, except the pistachios, and blend to a paste in a blender or food processor. Strain through a muslin or cheesecloth–lined sieve.
2 Add the remaining milk to the strained mixture and check for sweetness. Chill for 3 to 4 hours to allow the flavors to combine and serve in tall glasses, each garnished with a little ground pistachio.

Serves 4   Preparation Time: 20 mins
Chilling Time: 4 hours

Savory Cumin Drink
Jal Jeera

2 tablespoons black cumin seeds
2 teaspoons dried mango powder (amchoor)
1 teaspoon ground ginger
$^{1}/_{2}$ teaspoon black peppercorns
$1^{1}/_{2}$ teaspoons dried mint
$^{1}/_{2}$ teaspoon ground red pepper
$^{1}/_{4}$ teaspoon carom seeds (ajwain)
$^{1}/_{4}$ teaspoon asafoetida powder
4 cloves
$1^{1}/_{2}$ teaspoons rock salt
1 teaspoon salt
Fresh mint leaves, to garnish (optional)

1 Dry-roast all the ingredients in a nonstick wok or skillet over low heat, stirring continuously for 3 to 4 minutes until fragrant. Allow to cool, then grind to a powder in a blender or mortar and pestle. Keep in a tightly covered jar. To prepare the drink, mix 1 teaspoon of this powder with 1 glass of hot or iced water. Add 1 teaspoon Mint Coriander Chutney (page 26) and $^{1}/_{4}$ teaspoon sugar to each glass. Garnish the drink with fresh mint leaves.

Serves 4   Preparation Time: 15 mins
Cooking Time: 5 mins

Miscellaneous

Onion, Tomato and Cucumber Relish
Kachumber

1 medium onion, finely diced
2 medium tomatoes, finely diced
3 tablespoons (30 g) finely diced cucumber
1 tablespoon minced coriander leaves (cilantro)
1 green chili, deseeded and minced
$^{1}/_{4}$ teaspoon ground red pepper
$^{1}/_{2}$ teaspoon salt
$^{1}/_{2}$ cup (125 ml) lemon juice

1 Mix together the onions, tomatoes, cucumber, coriander, green chili and red pepper. Immediately before serving, stir in the salt and lemon juice and serve with Dhansak Dal (page 101) or any other Indian meal.

Preparation Time: 15 mins

Homemade Paneer

4 cups (1 liter) fresh milk
1 tablespoon of lemon juice or 1 tablespoon white vinegar

1 Bring the milk slowly to a boil in a heavy-bottomed saucepan, stirring occasionally. Remove from heat and stir in the lemon juice while the milk is still hot, stirring vigorously until the milk starts to curdle.
2 Strain through a muslin or cheesecloth until all the whey or liquid has drained off. The curds left are known as chenna. Knead the curds lightly until smooth.
3 Wrap the curds in the muslin or cheesecloth, then shape it into an oblong or a square. Wrap tightly and place it under a heavy weight for 1 to 2 hours to compress it.
4 Remove the weight and cut the paneer into the desired shape. Paneer can be kept for 3 to 4 days if stored in an airtight container in the refrigerator.

Mint and Cucumber Raita

$^{1}/_{2}$ cup (25 g) mint leaves
$^{1}/_{2}$ cup (25 g) coriander leaves (cilantro)
1 baby cucumber, diced
2 teaspoons grated ginger
1 teaspoon minced green chilies
1 cup (250 g) yogurt
$^{1}/_{4}$ teaspoon salt
$^{1}/_{4}$ teaspoon freshly ground black pepper

1 Mince the mint and coriander leaves and combine with the cucumber, ginger and green chilies.
2 Whisk the yogurt in a bowl, add the mint mixture, salt and pepper and mix well. Serve as an accompaniment to any Indian meal.

Preparation Time: 15 minutes

Vegetable Samosas

7 tablespoons (100 g) ghee or butter
2 cups (250 g) flour
$1/2$ teaspoon carom seeds (*ajwain*)
$1/2$ teaspoon salt
$2/3$ cup (150 ml) water
Oil for deep-frying

Filling
8 oz (250 g) potatoes
2 tablespoons oil
$1/2$ teaspoon cumin seeds
$1/3$ cup (50 g) fresh or frozen green peas, cooked
$1/2$ teaspoon salt
1 teaspoon ground coriander
$1/2$ teaspoon ground turmeric
$1/2$–1 teaspoon ground red pepper
1 green chili, deseeded and minced
1 teaspoon dried mango powder (*amchoor*)

1 Rub the ghee or butter into the flour until the mixture is crumbly. Mix in the carom seeds and salt, then gradually add the water to make a firm but pliable dough. Leave for 30 minutes, covered with a damp cloth.
2 Prepare the Filling by boiling the potatoes in a pot of salted water until tender. Cut the potatoes into small cubes. Heat the oil and stir-fry the cumin seeds in a nonstick skillet for about 1 minute until they begin to crackle. Add the remaining ingredients and continue stir-frying for 1 minute. Set aside to cool.
3 Roll out the pastry thinly, then cut into circles, 3 in (6 cm) in diameter. Cut each circle in half. Place a spoonful of Filling in the center of one semi-circle of pastry. Fold the two ends of the semi-circle over the Filling to form a triangle, pressing the edges together to seal firmly.
4 Heat the oil in a wok and deep-fry the samosas for about 5 minutes until golden brown. Serve hot with Mint Coriander Chutney (page 26).

Makes 8 pieces   Preparation time: 15 mins + 30 mins resting time
Cooking time: 15 mins

Deep-fried Banana and Potato Fritters   Kele Ka Tikka

1 teaspoon coriander seeds
7 oz (200 g) unripe bananas
12 oz (350 g) boiled potatoes, mashed
1 teaspoon Chaat Masala (page 23)
$1/4$ teaspoon Garam Masala (page 23)
$1/2$ teaspoon salt
2 tablespoons minced ginger
1 heaped tablespoon minced coriander leaves (cilantro)
2 green chilies, deseeded and minced
1 heaped tablespoon cornstarch
$3 1/2$ oz (100 g) fine wheat or rice vermicelli, broken into small pieces
Oil for deep-frying

1 Dry-roast the coriander seeds in a nonstick wok or skillet, stirring continuously for 1 to 2 minutes until fragrant. Allow to cool, then grind to a powder in a blender or mortar and pestle.
2 Steam the bananas in the skins until soft, then cool. Remove the skins and grate the bananas. Combine the grated bananas with the remaining ingredients, except for the vermicelli and oil. Mix well, then shape the mixture into balls and roll in the vermicelli, pressing lightly to make sure the vermicelli adheres.
3 Heat the oil in a wok and deep-fry the balls until they are golden brown.

Serves 4   Preparation time: 25 mins   Cooking time: 10 mins

Pakora   Batter-coated Vegetable Fritters

2 medium potatoes (9 oz/250 g)
1 large or 2 small slender Asian eggplants
1 large onion
2 cups (250 g) chickpea flour or *besan*
1 teaspoon salt
1 teaspoon ground red pepper
$3/4$ teaspoon baking soda (bicarbonate of soda)
$3/4$ cup (175 ml) cold water
Oil for deep-frying

1 Peel the potatoes, halve them lengthwise, then cut in slices about $1/4$ in (5 mm) thick. Do not peel the eggplant, but slice in the same thickness as the potatoes. Peel, then slice the onion in the same thickness as the potatoes. Set the vegetables aside.
2 Combine the chickpea flour, salt, red pepper and baking soda, mixing well. Add the cold water to make a very thick batter of coating consistency.
3 Dip the vegetables, one at a time, into the batter, coating thoroughly. Heat the oil in a wok until very hot and deep-fry for 5 to 6 minutes until golden brown and cooked on the inside. Drain and set aside. Serve hot.

Serves 4   Preparation time: 20 mins   Cooking time: 20 mins

Relief!!!

from that
t you can it

EFRIGER TORS

ORS

Oh, to be
playing on Grass
Courts — at home!

Diced Chicken Masala on Toast

These two Anglo-Indian dishes are very mildly spiced and served, British-style, on hot toast.

$^1/_4$ cup (60 g) yogurt
1 teaspoon chili paste or minced
  fresh chilies
$^1/_2$ teaspoon Garam Masala (page 23)
$^1/_2$ teaspoon crushed garlic
$^1/_2$ teaspoon minced ginger
1 tablespoon lemon juice
8 oz (250 g) boneless chicken, diced
$1^1/_2$ tablespoons oil or butter
1 medium onion, sliced
$^1/_4$ teaspoon ground coriander
1 teaspoon ground red pepper
$^1/_2$ teaspoon ground turmeric
$^1/_2$ tablespoon curry powder
1 teaspoon paprika
5 medium tomatoes, or $^1/_2$ can (8
  oz/225 g) whole tomatoes, diced
2 tablespoons minced coriander
  leaves (cilantro)
$^1/_4$ teaspoon salt
$^1/_4$ teaspoon ground black pepper

1 In a large bowl, combine the yogurt, chili paste, Garam Masala, $^1/_4$ teaspoon garlic, $^1/_4$ teaspoon ginger and lemon juice with the chicken. Mix thoroughly and marinate for 30 minutes.
2 Heat the oil in a skillet and stir-fry the onions until lightly browned. Add the spices and the remaining garlic and ginger, and continue to stir-fry for 2 to 3 minutes until fragrant. Add the chicken (and any marinade), stir for 1 minute, then add the tomatoes. Simmer uncovered until the chicken is tender.
3 Remove the chicken and simmer the sauce until it has thickened. Remove the sauce from the heat and stir in the coriander and chicken. Season with salt and pepper and serve warm, spread on hot buttered toast.

Serves 4   Preparation time: 15 mins + 30 minutes marinating time
Cooking time: 30 mins

Chopped Masala Chicken Livers on Toast

1 tablespoon oil
2 medium onions, sliced
1 cup (300 g) chicken livers, rinsed
  and chopped
$^1/_2$ teaspoon ground red pepper
$^1/_2$ teaspoon ground coriander
$^1/_2$ teaspoon Garam Masala (page 23)
$^1/_2$ teaspoon grated ginger
1 medium tomato, blanched, peeled
  and diced
$^1/_4$ teaspoon salt
$^1/_4$ teaspoon ground black pepper
Minced coriander leaves (cilantro), to
  garnish

1 Heat the oil in a skillet and stir-fry the onions until transparent. Add the chicken livers and continue to stir-fry until the livers just start to change color.
2 Add the red pepper, coriander, Garam Masala and ginger, stir-fry for 2 minutes, then add the tomatoes. Cook over high heat for 5 minutes or until the livers are cooked and the sauce is reduced.
3 Liquidize in a blender for a smooth pâté or mash in the wok if you prefer a coarse texture. Season with salt and pepper, sprinkle with coriander leaves, and serve warm, spread on hot buttered toast.

Note: To remove the skin with ease, blanch the tomatoes in boiling water before peeling.

Serves 8   Preparation time: 15 mins   Cooking time: 15 mins

Mulligatawny Soup

The inspiration for this Anglo-Indian soup was southern Indian "pepper water" or *rasam*, which certainly did not include apple, curry powder and chicken. This flavorful soup is still a favorite among Westernized middle-class Indians, who enjoy it in their private clubs.

2 tablespoons oil
1 teaspoon minced ginger
3 cloves garlic, crushed
1 large onion, sliced
2 tablespoons chickpea flour or *besan*
1 green apple, peeled and diced
1 teaspoon ground cumin
1 teaspoon ground coriander
$1/2$ teaspoon ground turmeric
$1/2$ teaspoon ground cloves
2 medium tomatoes, blanched, peeled and diced
1 bay leaf or 1 teaspoon thyme
1 teaspoon coarsely ground black pepper
1 teaspoon ground red pepper
3 cups (750 ml) chicken stock or 2 chicken stock
 cubes dissolved in 3 cups (750 ml) boiling water
$1/2$ cup (125 ml) coconut cream or 1 cup (250 ml) milk (optional)
1–2 tablespoons boiled rice (optional)
1 cup (125 g) cooked chicken, shredded
Lemon wedges, to serve

1 Heat the oil in a saucepan, add the ginger and garlic and stir-fry for 2 minutes. Add the onion and stir-fry until the onion is transparent.
2 Add the chickpea flour, apple, cumin, coriander, turmeric, cloves, tomatoes, bay leaf, black pepper, red pepper, chicken stock and coconut cream. Bring to a boil, cover, then reduce the heat to low.
3 Simmer for 45 minutes then process in a blender. Add the rice, if using, and chicken, stir well and serve with lemon wedges.

Serves 4   Preparation time: 20 mins   Cooking time: 1 hour

Fragrant Yogurt Soup   Raab

1 tablespoon oil
$1/_2$ teaspoon black mustard seeds
2 green chilies, minced
$1/_2$ teaspoon crushed garlic
$1/_4$ teaspoon grated ginger
$3/_4$ cup (190 g) yogurt
3 cups (750 ml) chicken or vegetable
   stock or 2 chicken stock cubes in 3
   cups of boiling water
$1/_4$ teaspoon salt
Pinch of ground turmeric
Pinch of ground red pepper
1 teaspoon minced coriander leaves
   (cilantro)
$1/_2$ teaspoon minced mint leaves
Few drops of chili oil, to garnish
   (optional)

1 Heat the oil in a saucepan and stir-fry the mustard seeds for about 1 minute until they crackle. Add the green chilies, garlic and ginger. Stir-fry for 5 minutes, then add the yogurt, chicken stock and salt.
2 Simmer over low heat for 10 to 15 minutes, stirring constantly to prevent the yogurt from curdling. Add the turmeric, red pepper, coriander and mint leaves, mix well and serve hot, sprinkled with a few drops of chili oil.

Serves 4   Preparation time: 20 mins   Cooking time: 20 mins

Spiced Lentil Rasam Soup   Nimma Rasam

1 cup (200 g) yellow lentils (*tuvar dal*)
10 cups ($2^1/_2$ liters) water
3 tablespoons oil
2 teaspoons black mustard seeds
6 cloves garlic, crushed
20 curry leaves
2 dried chilies, cut into pieces
12 whole black peppercorns,
   coarsely crushed
2 pinches of ground turmeric
2 pinches of asafoetida powder
3 very ripe medium tomatoes,
   quartered
1 teaspoon salt
$1/_2$ cup (125 ml) lemon juice
Minced coriander leaves (cilantro),
   to garnish

Rasam Masala
1 teaspoon coriander seeds
$1/_2$ teaspoon cumin seeds
$1/_2$ teaspoon fenugreek seeds
1 teaspoon black peppercorns
1 teaspoon black mustard seeds
3 dried chilies, broken into pieces
10 curry leaves
Pinch of asafoetida powder

1 Prepare the Rasam Masala by dry-roasting all the ingredients, except the asafoetida, in a nonstick wok or skillet over low heat, stirring continuously for 2 to 3 minutes until the chilies are crisp and the spices fragrant. Take care not to burn. Allow to cool, then grind to a powder in a blender or mortar and pestle. Mix in the asafoetida powder.
2 Wash the lentils and simmer in the water for 30 to 40 minutes until they disintegrate. Strain the lentils, reserving some of the liquid. Purée the lentils with some of the reserved liquid, return the purée to the pot and continue to simmer on low heat.
3 Meanwhile, heat the oil in a wok and stir-fry the mustard seeds for 1 minute until the seeds begin to crackle. Add the garlic, curry leaves, chilies, crushed peppercorns, turmeric and asafoetida and continue to stir-fry. Pour the fried spices into the pot of puréed lentils, then add the tomatoes, salt, Rasam Masala and lemon juice. Simmer for a few minutes and serve hot, garnished with coriander leaves.

Serves 4–6   Preparation time: 20 mins   Cooking time: 50 mins

Chapati   Unleavened Flatbreads

For the best results, chapati should be properly kneaded; using slow speed and a plastic blade in a food processor is an acceptable alternative to 10 to 15 minutes of hand-kneading

2 cups (250 g) very fine whole wheat (wholemeal) flour, or plain flour
3/4 cup (175 ml) warm water
2 teaspoons softened ghee or butter

1 Sift the flour into a bowl, gradually adding the water and mixing together with your fingertips. The dough should be pliable, yet not too sticky. Mix in the ghee or butter. Turn the dough out onto a floured board or place in a food processor. Knead by hand for 10 to 15 minutes or process on low speed for 5 minutes. Roll the dough into a ball, cover with a damp cloth and set aside to rest for at least 1 hour.
2 Knead the dough again for 3 to 4 minutes, then divide the dough into twelve balls of equal size. On a lightly floured surface, flatten the balls with your hands, then roll them out into flat circles.
3 Heat a nonstick skillet until very hot, place a piece of dough in the skillet and cook for 1 minute until brown spots appear underneath. Turn over and cook for 1 more minute on the other side, pressing the top of the chapati with a clean cloth to help air bubbles form and to keep the chapati light. As each chapati is cooked, wrap it in a clean cloth to keep warm. Serve with Bean and Lentil Stew (page 49) or Gujarati Spiced Vegetables with Coconut (page 51).

Makes 12 pieces   Preparation time: 15 mins + 1 hour resting time
Cooking time: 5 mins

Puri   Deep-fried Bread Puffs

Puri are a delicious alternative to chapati and exactly the same dough is used. To ensure they puff up when cooking, keep flicking the hot oil over the top while the puri are cooking.

1 quantity of chapati dough
Oil for deep-frying

1 Roll out the dough as for the chapati and divide into twelve balls of equal size. On a lightly floured surface, flatten the balls with your palms, then roll them out into flat circles.
2 Heat plenty of oil in a wok until very hot. Place one circle of dough into the wok and immediately start flicking hot oil over the top of it with a spatula so that it swells up like a ball. This should only take a few seconds. Turn and continue to deep-fry on the other side until golden brown. Repeat with the rest of the dough. Serve immediately with a curry, such as Creamy Shrimp Curry (page 75).

Makes 12 pieces   Preparation time: 15 mins   Cooking time: 5 mins

Tandoori Naan   Leavened Flatbreads

The characteristic tear-drop shape of this bread is obtained by the way the dough droops as it cooks on the wall of a tandoor.

4 cups (500 g) flour
$1/2$ teaspoon baking powder
1 teaspoon salt
$1/2$ teaspoon yeast
2 tablespoons lukewarm water
$1/2$ cup (125 ml) milk
1 tablespoon sugar
1 egg
4 tablespoons oil
1 teaspoon nigella seeds (*kalonji*)

1 Sift the flour, baking powder and salt into a mixing bowl and make a well in the center. In another bowl, mix the yeast and lukewarm water together, then add the milk, sugar, egg and 2 tablespoons of the oil. Pour this into the center of the sifted flour and knead, adding more water if necessary to form a soft dough. Add the remaining oil, knead again, then cover with a damp cloth and place in a warm, dry place for 15 minutes to allow the dough to rise.
2 Knead the dough again, cover and leave for another 2 to 3 hours. About half an hour before the naan is required, turn the oven to high heat. Divide the dough into eight balls and let them rest for 3 to 5 minutes. While the dough is resting, sprinkle a baking sheet with the nigella seeds and place it in the oven to heat.
3 Shape each ball of dough into an elongated oval shape by flattening and stretching the dough. Turn on the broiler or grill, remove the baking sheet from the oven and place 2 or 3 pieces of dough onto the preheated sheet. Place the sheet several inches under the broiler and bake the naan until they are puffed up and golden brown. Serve hot.

Makes 8 pieces   Preparation time: 20 + 3 hours standing time   Cooking time: 10 mins

Lucchi   Bengali Fried Breads

Lucchi are similar to *puri*, except for the addition of semolina, for texture, and fennel for fragrance.

1 cup (125 g) flour
$1/2$ teaspoon salt
1 tablespoon fine semolina
1 teaspoon fennel seeds, dry-roasted
  in a skillet and ground
1 tablespoon oil
$1/4$ cup (60 ml) water
Ghee or oil for deep-frying

1 Sift the flour and salt into a large bowl, add the semolina and fennel seeds and mix well. In another bowl, combine the oil and water and mix together with the dry ingredients. Knead well to make a smooth dough, adding more water if necessary. Cover the bowl with a cloth and set the dough aside for 15 minutes.
2 Divide the dough into eight balls, flatten slightly, then roll them out in the shape of disks that are 4 to 5 in (10 to 12 cm) in diameter.
3 Heat the ghee or oil in a wok until very hot, then deep-fry the breads, one at a time, flicking the hot ghee or oil over the top so that it puffs up. Turn and cook on the other side until golden brown.

Serves 4   Preparation time: 15 mins + 15 mins standing time   Cooking time: 10 mins

Dosai Southern Indian Rice flour Pancakes

A southern Indian breakfast favorite, these tangy pancakes are often served with Fresh Coconut Chutney and Tomato Chutney, with a spicy *dal* soup on the side, like Yellow Lentil and Tomato Stew. They can also be stuffed with spiced potatoes to make Masala Dosai.

$1^{1}/_{2}$ cups (300 g) uncooked long-grain rice
$^{1}/_{2}$ cup (220 g) white lentils (*urad dal*)
$^{1}/_{2}$ teaspoon salt
$^{1}/_{2}$ onion, halved
$1^{1}/_{2}$ tablespoons oil

1 Place the rice and lentils into separate bowls, cover each with water and soak overnight. Grind the rice and lentils separately in a blender or food processor, adding a little water if necessary to obtain a smooth consistency.
2 Mix the ground rice and lentils together and leave at room temperature overnight to ferment. The batter can now be refrigerated for up to 24 hours until required. Stir the batter, adding salt and sufficient water to achieve the consistency of a very thick cream.
3 Heat a nonstick skillet or griddle and rub with half an onion. Grease lightly with a little of the oil and pour in a ladle ($^{1}/_{4}$ cup/60 ml) of batter, smearing it quickly with the back of the ladle to form a thin pancake that is 5 to 6 in (12 to 15 cm) in diameter. Cook for 2 to 3 minutes until the bottom is golden brown and the top starts to set. Turn over and cook on the other side, then serve hot with Fresh Coconut Chutney (page 25) and Yellow Lentil and Tomato Stew (page 49).

Note: If desired, stuff the dosai with hot spiced potato, or with some chicken masala spread for a non-vegetarian treat.

Serves 4–6   Preparation time: 10 mins + 24 hours soaking and fermenting time
Cooking time: 30 mins

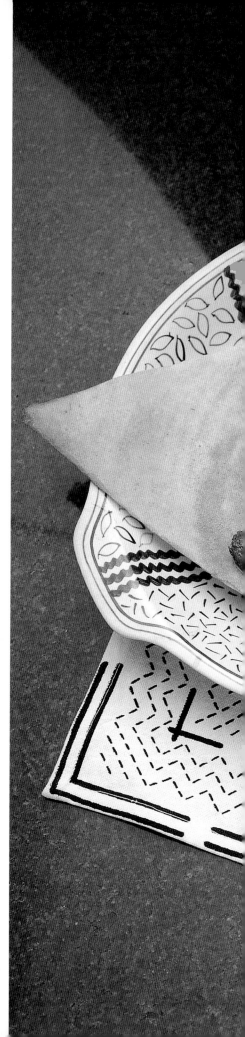

Appam   Rice Pancakes

3 cups (600 g) uncooked rice
3 tablespoons white lentils (*urad dal*)
2 cups (500 ml) coconut milk
$1/2$ teaspoon baking soda (bicarbonate of soda)
1 teaspoon salt
Oil, to grease

1 Soak the rice and white lentils in water for 4 hours. Drain, then place in a blender or food processor and grind to a thick paste. Leave to ferment overnight.
2 Add the coconut milk, baking soda and salt to the paste, and beat thoroughly to mix.
3 Grease a small heavy nonstick wok over low heat. Pour in a ladle of the batter, grab both sides of the wok and swirl the batter so that it spreads evenly in the shape of a circle, over the base of the wok. Cook on low heat for 2 minutes, or until bubbles form on the surface. The edges should be crispy and the center thick and moist. Serve with Fresh Coconut Chutney (page 25) and Yellow Lentil and Tomato Stew (page 49).

Serves 4   Preparation time: 15 mins + overnight fermenting time
Cooking time: 20 mins

Paratha   Flaky Fried Flatbreads

These wonderfully light breads are normally flung out in circles, like a fisherman throwing his net (*vecchu*), until paper thin. They can be hand-pulled like strudel for a similar result.

$3^1/_3$ cups (420 g) flour
1 teaspoon salt
3 eggs, lightly beaten
1 cup (250 ml) water
$3/_4$ cup (180 ml) vegetable oil

1 Sift the flour and salt into a bowl. Make a well in the center of the flour, pour in the beaten eggs and mix together, using your fingertips. Gradually add the water and combine to make a very soft dough. Knead for 10 minutes. Divide the dough evenly into 10 balls, cover with a damp cloth and leave to stand for 30 minutes.
2 Spread out each ball on a well-oiled tabletop, flatten with the palm of your hand and pull the edges of the dough gently to stretch it out as wide and as thin as possible. Fold the dough in half, brush the surface with oil and fold in half again. Roll each piece of dough into a curled ball and leave to rest for 15 minutes. Flatten each ball with the palm of your hand again, then use a rolling pin to shape the dough into flat circles.
3 Oil a griddle or skillet and cook for 1 to 2 minutes, or until the bottom turns golden brown. Turn and cook on the other side for another 1 to 2 minutes. Serve hot with Bean and Lentil Stew (page 49) or Mild Chicken Curry (page 81).

Makes 10 pieces   Preparation time: 25 mins + 45 mins standing time
Cooking time: 10 mins

Lemon Rice Chitrannam

1¹/₂ cups (300 g) uncooked long-
  grain rice (preferably Basmati),
  washed and drained
3 cups (750 ml) water
1 teaspoon Bengal gram (*channa
  dal*) or yellow split peas
1 tablespoon split raw cashew nuts
1 tablespoon oil
1 teaspoon black mustard seeds
Pinch of asafoetida powder
10 curry leaves
¹/₂ teaspoon minced ginger
¹/₂ green chili, minced
2–3 dried chilies, broken into pieces
1 teaspoon white lentils (*urad dal*)
¹/₂ teaspoon ground turmeric
3 tablespoons lemon juice
1–1¹/₂ teaspoons salt
1 tablespoon water
Fresh coriander leaves (cilantro),
  to garnish

1 Boil the rice in the water for 15 to 20 minutes until the grains are just tender. Drain thoroughly and set aside.
2 Dry-roast the Bengal gram and cashew nuts in a nonstick wok for 2 to 3 minutes until lightly toasted. Remove from the wok and set aside.
3 Heat the oil in the wok and stir-fry the mustard seeds for 1 minute until the seeds begin to pop. Add the asafoetida, curry leaves, ginger, chilies, Bengal gram, cashews, lentils and turmeric. Continue to stir-fry, then add the lemon juice, salt and water. Simmer for 2 to 3 minutes, toss in the rice and heat through. Garnish with coriander leaves and serve with a few poppadums, chutneys and Mint and Cucumber Raita (page 27).

Serves 4–6   Preparation time: 20 mins   Cooking time: 35 mins

Coconut Rice Thengai Sadam

1¹/₃ cups (250 g) uncooked Basmati
  or long-grain rice, washed and
  drained
3 cups (750 ml) water
3 tablespoons oil
1 teaspoon black mustard seeds
3–5 dried chilies, broken into pieces
2 green chilies, sliced
1–2 cloves garlic, minced
¹/₂ tablespoon minced ginger
1 teaspoon white lentils (*urad dal*)
2 tablespoons Bengal gram (*channa
  dal*) or yellow split peas
10 curry leaves
Pinch of ground turmeric
Pinch of asafoetida powder
1 teaspoon salt
¹/₂ cup (50 g) freshly grated coconut,
  dry-roasted in a skillet until golden
  brown
Fresh coriander leaves (cilantro), to
  garnish

1 Boil the rice in the water for 5 minutes, drain well, then spread out on a tray to cool.
2 Heat the oil in a wok and stir-fry the mustard seeds, chilies, garlic and ginger for 1 minute until the seeds begin to pop. Add the white lentils, Bengal gram, curry leaves and turmeric and stir-fry until the lentils turn golden. Add the asafoetida, salt, coconut and rice and mix thoroughly.
3 Remove from the heat and set the rice aside for 1 hour to allow the flavors to penetrate. Reheat and serve garnished with coriander and, if desired, a few shreds of fresh coconut. Ideal with a few poppadums, chutneys and yogurt.

Serves 4   Preparation time: 15 mins + 1 hour standing time   Cooking time: 20 mins

Vegetable Pulao　Sabzi Pulao

Ideal for vegetarians, this dish can include additional vegetables such as green peas or small pieces of cauliflower, if desired.

1¹/₂ cups (300 g) uncooked long-
　grain rice (preferably Basmati)
1 tablespoon ghee or butter
1 teaspoon cumin seeds
1 cinnamon stick (2 in/5 cm)
5 green cardamom pods, bruised
7 cloves
1 medium onion, diced
1 tablespoon yogurt
2 medium tomatoes, diced
1 cup (170g) diced, cooked potatoes
1 cup (100 g) finely sliced green
　beans
1 cup (120 g) diced carrot
Pinch of saffron threads, soaked in 1
　tablespoon of hot milk for 15 minutes
1 teaspoon ground turmeric
1 teaspoon ground coriander
3 cups (750 ml) water
1¹/₂ teaspoons salt
Fresh coriander leaves (cilantro), to
　garnish

1 Wash the rice in a pot, leaving enough water to just cover the rice and soak for 30 minutes. Drain and set aside.
2 Heat the ghee in a wok and stir-fry the cumin, cinnamon, cardamom and cloves for 1 minute until they begin to crackle. Add the onion and stir-fry until golden, then add the yogurt, vegetables, saffron, turmeric, coriander and ¹/₂ cup (125 ml) of water. Cover and simmer for 3 minutes.
3 Add 2¹/₂ cups (625 ml) of water, the drained rice and salt. Stir, bring to a boil, then simmer uncovered for about 10 minutes until the water is completely absorbed.
4 Cover the wok with a damp towel, then cover with the lid, and cook over very low heat for 5 to 10 minutes. Remove from the heat, keep covered and leave to stand for 15 to 20 minutes. Stir gently with a fork and serve garnished with coriander leaves.

Serves 4　Preparation time: 15 mins + 30 mins soaking time　Cooking time: 45 mins

Rice and Lentils　Tuvar Dal Khichdee

The inspiration for Anglo-Indian "kedgeree," this is a simple mixture of rice and lentils.

¹/₂ cup (100 g) uncooked rice
3 tablespoons yellow lentils (*tuvar dal*)
　or Bengal gram (*channa dal*) or
　green mung beans (*moong dal*)
1 cinnamon stick (2 in/5 cm)
2 cloves
2 cardamom pods, bruised
1¹/₂ cups (375 ml) water
1 teaspoon salt
1 tablespoon oil
¹/₂ teaspoon cumin seeds
1–2 green chilies (optional)
Pinch of asafoetida powder
1 teaspoon ground turmeric

1 Wash the rice and the lentils. If using yellow lentils or Bengal gram, simmer them in water until just soft, then drain. This step is not necessary if using green mung beans.
2 Combine the lentils with the rice, cinnamon stick, cloves, cardamom pods, water and salt. Cover and simmer over low heat for about 1 hour until very soft. Add water to the pot if the mixture thickens too much.
3 Heat the oil in a wok or skillet and stir-fry the cumin seeds, chilies, asafoetida and turmeric for 1 minute until they begin to crackle. Pour over the top of the cooked rice and serve hot.

Serves 4　Preparation time: 15 mins　Cooking time: 1 hour

Bean and Lentil Stew   Dal Maharani

$^1/_2$ cup (90 g) Black gram lentils (*urad dal*)
2 tablespoons (30 g) dried pinto or kidney beans
1 in (2$^1/_2$ cm) ginger, sliced
1 teaspoon salt
1 tablespoon ghee or butter
1 teaspoon cumin seeds
1–2 green chilies, slit lengthwise
2 medium tomatoes, diced
2 teaspoons Garam Masala (page 23)
$^1/_2$ cup (125 ml) cream

1 Rinse and soak the Black gram lentils and beans overnight. Combine the lentils and beans in a saucepan with the ginger, salt and enough water to cover. Bring to a boil, cover and simmer over low heat for 1 to 1$^1/_4$ hours or until just soft.
2 Heat the ghee or butter in a skillet, add the cumin seeds and chilies and stir-fry for 1 minute until the cumin seeds crackle. Add to the cooked lentils and beans, along with the diced tomatoes and half the Garam Masala. Simmer for 10 minutes until the tomatoes soften.
3 Keep aside 1 tablespoon of the cream and stir the rest into the lentil stew. Stir gently to allow the cream to heat through then serve in individual bowls with a few drops of the remaining cream and a sprinkling of the Garam Masala. Serve with some Tandoori Naan (page 39) or Paratha (page 43).

Serves 4   Preparation time: 10 mins + overnight soaking   Cooking time: 1 hour 30 mins

Yellow Lentil and Tomato Stew   Sambar Dal

1$^1/_2$ cups (300 g) yellow lentils (*toor dal*), rinsed and drained
8 cups (2 liters) water
1 teaspoon ground turmeric
6 medium tomatoes, diced
2 medium onions, diced
3 tablespoons sambar powder
3 tablespoons tamarind pulp, soaked in 3 tablespoons water, mashed and strained
20 curry leaves
$^3/_4$ teaspoon salt
Fresh coriander leaves (cilantro), to garnish

1 Combine the lentils, water and turmeric in a pot and bring to a boil. Reduce the heat to low and simmer for about 30 minutes, partially covered, or until the lentils are soft.
2 Add the diced tomatoes and onion and continue to simmer for another 15 minutes, stirring occasionally until the tomatoes turn pulpy. Add the sambar powder, tamarind juice, curry leaves and salt and bring to a boil. Stir in the coriander leaves and serve with Dosai (page 40).

Serves 6–8   Preparation time:10 mins   Cooking time: 45 mins

Grilled Paneer Tikka with Mint and Coriander

$^1/_2$ lb (250 g) Homemade Paneer
  (page 27)
2–3 tablespoons Mint Coriander
  Chutney (page 26)
$^1/_2$ cup (125 g) hung yogurt (page 21)
$1^1/_2$ teaspoons crushed garlic
$1^1/_2$ teaspoons crushed ginger
1 teaspoon ground turmeric
1 teaspoon ground white pepper
1 teaspoon Garam Masala (page 23)
1 teaspoon salt
$1^1/_2$ tablespoons oil
2 tablespoons lemon juice
Sliced onions and lemon wedges,
  to serve

1 Cut the paneer into squares about $^3/_4$ in (2 cm) thick. With a knife, make 3 to 4 shallow cuts into one side of each paneer and gently push about $^1/_4$ teaspoon of the Mint Coriander Chutney into the shallow cuts.
2 Mix all the remaining ingredients together to make a marinade and rub onto the pieces of paneer. Leave to marinate for 45 minutes to 1 hour.
3 Skewer the paneer and bake in a very hot oven or under a very hot grill for 4 minutes, or until the paneer starts to brown. Serve with sliced raw onion and lemon wedges.

Serves 4   Preparation time: 20 mins + 1 hour marinating time   Cooking time: 10 mins

Gujarati Spiced Vegetables with Coconut   Undiya

2 tablespoons oil
1 teaspoon cumin seeds
$^1/_2$ teaspoon carom seeds (*ajwain*)
Pinch of asafoetida powder
$^1/_3$ cup (75 g) red lentils (*masoor dal*),
  soaked 4 hours in warm water, then
  drained
$^1/_3$ cup (75 g) diced tomatoes
$^1/_3$ cup (60 g) peeled and diced
  potatoes
$^1/_3$ cup (60 g) diced eggplant
$^1/_3$ cup (60 g) peeled and diced sweet
  potatoes
$^1/_3$ cup (60 g) peeled and diced purple
  or white yam (optional)
$^1/_3$ cup (60 g) peeled and diced plan-
  tain (optional)
2 tablespoons freshly grated or moistened unsweetened desiccated
  coconut, to garnish

Masala
2 tablespoons coriander seeds
1 teaspoon cumin seeds
$^1/_2$ teaspoon carom seeds (*ajwain*)
2 tablespoons raw peanuts
$^2/_3$ cup (150 ml) water
4–7 green chilies, sliced
2 tablespoons roughly chopped
  coriander leaves (cilantro)
1 teaspoon crushed garlic
1 teaspoon minced ginger
1 tablespoon freshly grated coconut
  or moistened unsweetened desiccated coconut
$^1/_2$ tablespoon shaved palm sugar or
  dark brown sugar (optional)
1 teaspoon salt

1 First prepare the Masala by dry-roasting the coriander, cumin, carom and peanuts in a nonstick wok or skillet for 1 to 2 minutes, stirring until the spices crackle. Allow to cool, then place in a blender or food processor with the water and grind to a paste. Add the remaining Masala ingredients and blend or process until smooth.
2 Heat the oil in a wok and stir-fry the cumin, carom and asafoetida for 1 minute until the spices begin to crackle. Add the Masala paste and stir-fry for 5 minutes. Add the tomatoes and continue cooking for several minutes until the tomatoes soften.
3 Add the drained lentils and the prepared vegetables. Cover the wok and simmer gently over medium heat for 10 to 15 minutes until the vegetables are tender. Sprinkle with freshly grated coconut and serve.

Serves 4–6   Preparation time: 1 hour + 4 hours soaking time   Cooking time: 30 mins

Vegetarian Paneer Shashlik

$^1/_2$ lb (250 g) Homemade Paneer
  (page 27)
2 green or red bell peppers
2 medium onions
2 medium tomatoes
1 cup (100 g) pineapple chunks
8 button mushrooms
Oil to brush the skewers

Marinade
3 tablespoons yogurt
1 tablespoon oil
1 teaspoon tomato paste
1 teaspoon salt
1 teaspoon ground red pepper
1 teaspoon ground coriander
1 teaspoon ground cumin

1 Combine all the Marinade ingredients. Cut the paneer, peppers, onions and tomatoes into chunks of roughly equal size, add the pineapple and mix thoroughly with the Marinade. Leave to marinate for 1 hour, then thread the ingredients onto skewers.

2 Cook in a hot oven, under a grill, or over a hot barbecue for 7 to 8 minutes on each side, brushing with oil and turning halfway through cooking.

Serves 6   Preparation time: 20 mins + 1 hour marinating time   Cooking time: 15 mins

Spiced Roasted Eggplant Baigan Bhartha

1 lb (500 g) eggplants
$1^1/_2$ tablespoons ghee or oil
2 medium onions, diced
$1^1/_2$ teaspoons ground coriander
2 teaspoons ground cumin
1 teaspoon ground red pepper
$^1/_2$ teaspoon Garam Masala (page 23)
3 medium tomatoes, blanched,
  peeled and diced
2 green chilies, deseeded and
  minced
1 teaspoon salt
$2^1/_2$ teaspoons minced coriander
  leaves (cilantro)

1 Rub the eggplants with a little oil and roast under a hot grill or broiler for several minutes on each side until the skin blackens and the eggplant is soft inside. Peel the eggplant, discard the skin, then slice and set aside.

2 Heat the ghee in a wok and stir-fry the onion until lightly browned. Add the coriander, cumin, red pepper and Garam Masala and stir-fry for 1 minute. Add the tomatoes and chili to the wok and continue to stir-fry for 2 to 3 minutes. Mix in the sliced eggplant and salt, and stir until dry. Sprinkle with coriander leaves.

Note: If using large Mediterranean eggplants, it may be necessary to halve or quarter them lengthwise first before roasting, so they evenly cook through.

Serves 4–6   Preparation time: 20 mins   Cooking time: 15 mins

Spicy Chickpea Dumplings in Yogurt Sauce   Kadhi Pakora

An ideal dish for vegetarians, this delicious Punjabi recipe consists of savory dumplings made from chickpea flour or *besan*, served in a yogurt sauce.

$3/4$ cup (100 g) chickpea flour or *besan*
1 medium onion, diced
1–2 green chilies, deseeded and minced
2 tablespoons minced ginger
1 tablespoon minced coriander leaves (cilantro)
1 teaspoon salt
$1/2$ teaspoon carom seeds (*ajwain*)
$1/4$ teaspoon baking soda (bicarbonate of soda)
$1/2$ cup (125 ml) water
Oil for deep-frying

Yogurt Sauce
2 tablespoons chickpea flour or *besan*
1 cup (250 g) yogurt
1 teaspoon salt
$1/2$ teaspoon ground turmeric
3 cups (750 ml) water
2 tablespoons oil
10 curry leaves
$1/2$ teaspoon black mustard seeds
3 dried chilies
$1/2$ teaspoon cumin seeds
$1/4$ teaspoon fenugreek seeds

1 First make the Yogurt Sauce by whisking the chickpea flour, yogurt, salt and turmeric together. Place the mixture in a pot with water and simmer for 25 minutes, stirring from time to time.
2 While the Yogurt Sauce is simmering, heat the oil in a wok or skillet over low to medium heat and stir-fry the curry leaves, mustard seeds, dried chilies, cumin and fenugreek for 1 to 2 minutes until the spices crackle and become fragrant. Add the spices to the simmering pot of Yogurt Sauce.
3 Mix all the ingredients for the dumplings (except the oil) in a bowl, gradually adding water to form a sticky consistency. Wet your hands, take a little of the dumpling mixture and shape the mixture into small bite-sized balls.
4 Heat the oil until it is very hot and deep-fry the dumplings, a few at a time, for 2 to 3 minutes until golden brown. Drain and place the dumplings in the yogurt sauce and simmer for 3 minutes. Serve hot with rice.

Serves 4–6   Preparation time: 15 mins   Cooking time: 35 mins

Spiced Chickpeas Pindi Channa

1 cup (200 g) chickpeas
1 tea bag
6 cups (1¹/₂ liters) water
2–3 tablespoons oil
2 medium onions, diced
2 teaspoons crushed garlic
2 tablespoons minced ginger
2 green chilies, sliced
3 medium tomatoes, diced
2 teaspoons ground coriander
1¹/₂ teaspoons ground cumin
¹/₂ teaspoon ground turmeric
1 teaspoon ground red pepper
1 teaspoon salt
2 teaspoons minced coriander leaves
  (cilantro)
¹/₄ teaspoon Garam Masala (page 23)
Shredded ginger, to garnish

1 Soak the chickpeas for 1 hour, then drain. Discard the liquid. Place the chickpeas, tea bag and water into a pot and simmer for 30 to 45 minutes until the chickpeas are tender. Drain, reserving 1 cup (250 ml) of the cooking liquid.

2 Heat the oil in a wok and stir-fry the onion until golden. Add the garlic, ginger and chilies and continue stir-frying for 5 minutes. Add the tomatoes, coriander, cumin, turmeric and red pepper, and stir-fry over low heat for 5 to 10 minutes until the oil separates.

3 Add the chickpeas, the reserved cooking liquid, salt and half the coriander leaves. Simmer uncovered for 15 to 20 minutes until the liquid has been absorbed, then add a pinch of Garam Masala and stir through. Serve with the remaining Garam Masala, coriander leaves and ginger shreds sprinkled on top.

Serves 4–6   Preparation time: 1 hour   Cooking time: 1 hour 20 mins

Curried Pinto Beans Rajmah

1 cup (200 g) dried pinto or kidney
  beans
5 cups (1¹/₄ liters) water
2–3 tablespoons oil
4 green cardamom pods, bruised
2 black cardamom pods, bruised
3 medium onions, diced
2 teaspoons crushed garlic
1 teaspoon grated ginger
1 teaspoon chili paste or minced
  fresh chilies
2¹/₂ teaspoons ground coriander
1 teaspoon ground cumin
1 teaspoon ground turmeric
2–3 medium tomatoes, diced
2 green chilies, sliced
2 tablespoons minced coriander
  leaves (cilantro)
1 teaspoon salt
1 teaspoon Garam Masala (page 23)

1 Rinse and soak the beans overnight. Drain, then simmer the beans in the water for 30 to 45 minutes until just tender. Drain, reserving 1 cup (250 ml) of the cooking liquid.

2 Heat the oil in a wok and stir-fry the cardamoms and onion until golden. Add the garlic, ginger and chili paste, and stir-fry for 5 minutes until the oil separates. Stir in the ground coriander, cumin and turmeric, and stir-fry over very low heat for 2 to 3 minutes. Add the tomatoes and continue stirring for another 2 minutes before adding the beans, reserved cooking liquid, chilies, half the coriander leaves and the salt.

3 Simmer uncovered until the beans are soft. Add half of the Garam Masala and continue simmering for 5 minutes. Serve with the remaining coriander leaves and Garam Masala.

Serves 4–6   Preparation time: 15 mins + overnight soaking time
Cooking time: 1 hour 20 mins

Mixed Vegetables with Yogurt and Fresh Coconut   Avial

2 cups (300 g) cubed pumpkin or any other firm vegetable like daikon radish or squash
2 medium potatoes, peeled
2 medium carrots, peeled
1 cup (180 g) green beans, cut into lengths
1 cup (250 g) whipped yogurt (page 21)
2 teaspoons plus 1 tablespoon ground cumin
1 teaspoon ground turmeric
2 cups (200 g) freshly grated coconut, or moistened unsweetened desiccated coconut
2–3 green chilies, sliced and deseeded
1–1$\frac{1}{2}$ teaspoons salt
1 tablespoon oil
1 teaspoon black mustard seeds
10 curry leaves

1 Wash the vegetables and cut into small cubes or strips. Place the vegetables in a pot with just enough water to cover, and simmer uncovered for about 10 minutes until half-cooked. Add the yogurt, 2 teaspoons cumin and the turmeric, simmer for 5 to 10 minutes, then add the grated coconut, 1 tablespoon cumin, chilies and salt. Mix well and leave over low heat.
2 Heat the oil in a wok and stir-fry the mustard seeds and curry leaves for 1 minute until the spices begin to crackle and become fragrant. Mix the mustard seeds and curry leaves into the vegetables, stir well and serve immediately.

Serves 4   Preparation time: 20 mins   Cooking time: 20 mins

Shredded Cabbage with Coconut and Spices   Muttakose Thuvial

1 tablespoon oil
2 dried chilies, broken into pieces and deseeded
1 teaspoon white lentils (*urad dal*)
1 teaspoon black mustard seeds
10 curry leaves
1 lb (500 g) cabbage, finely shredded
1 green chili, sliced
$\frac{1}{2}$ teaspoon ground red pepper (optional)
$\frac{1}{2}$ teaspoon ground turmeric
$\frac{1}{2}$ cup (40 g) freshly grated coconut or moistened unsweetened desiccated coconut
1 teaspoon salt, or more to taste
1 teaspoon minced coriander leaves (cilantro), to garnish

1 Heat the oil in a wok and stir-fry the dried chilies, lentils, mustard seeds and curry leaves for 1 to 2 minutes until the spices begin to crackle. Add the cabbage, chili, red pepper and turmeric, stirring to mix thoroughly.
2 Cover, lower the heat, and cook gently for 10 to 15 minutes, stirring occasionally, until the cabbage is just tender. Stir in the freshly grated coconut and season with salt. Garnish with coriander leaves and serve hot

Serves 4   Preparation time: 15 mins   Cooking time: 15 mins

Tandoori Baked Cauliflower and Stuffed Bell Peppers

The popularity of tandoor-baked dishes is so great in India that new recipes are being developed all the time, including this delicious and simple vegetable dish.

5–6 small bell peppers
1 medium cauliflower (about 1 lb/500 g)
1 teaspoon malt vinegar
1 teaspoon salt
1 teaspoon ground turmeric
$1/4$ teaspoon ground mace
$1/4$ teaspoon Chaat Masala (page 23)

Spicy Paneer Filling
1 teaspoon Garam Masala (page 23)
1 teaspoon Chaat Masala (page 23)
1 quantity of Homemade Paneer (page 27)

Marinade
$1^1/_2$ cups (375 g) hung yogurt (page 21)
2 teaspoons crushed garlic
$1^1/_2$ teaspoons grated ginger
$1^1/_2$ tablespoons chili paste or minced fresh chilies
$1/_2$ teaspoon Garam Masala (page 23)
$1^1/_2$ tablespoons oil
2 teaspoons malt vinegar

1 Cut the tops off the bell peppers, reserve the tops and scrape out the seeds from the inside of the bell peppers. Make the Spicy Paneer Filling by combining the ingredients together, then fill the bell peppers with the Spicy Paneer Filling. Set aside.
2 To prepare the Marinade, combine all the ingredients, then set aside.
3 Divide the cauliflower into florets, cut off the tougher part of the stem, and prick the thick tender stems with a fork to allow the seasonings to penetrate. Bring a pot of water to a boil and add the cauliflower, vinegar, salt and turmeric. Boil the cauliflower for 5 to 10 minutes until the cauliflower is just tender, then drain and allow to cool.
4 Coat the cauliflower and stuffed bell peppers with the Marinade, mix well and leave to marinate for $1^1/_2$ hours or overnight.
5 Place the cauliflower and stuffed bell peppers under a very hot grill or broiler for 5 to 6 minutes until tender and golden brown. Sprinkle with mace and Chaat Masala before serving hot. If desired, return the reserved tops of the bell peppers to the body of the bell peppers before serving.

Serves 4   Preparation time: 15 mins + 1 hour 30 mins marinating time
Cooking time: 20 mins

Spiced Potatoes in Yogurt   Dum Aloo

1¹/₂ lbs (700 g) baby new potatoes,
  halved
3 tablespoons oil
2 onions, diced
³/₄ cup (190 g) yogurt
4 black cardamom pods
1 teaspoon fennel seeds
1 cinnamon stick (2 in/5 cm)
2 tablespoons unsalted, roasted
  cashew nuts or shelled melon
  seeds, soaked in water
1¹/₂ tablespoons minced ginger
4 cloves garlic, minced
1¹/₂ teaspoons ground coriander
1 teaspoon ground cumin
1 teaspoon ground turmeric
¹/₂ teaspoon ground red pepper
¹/₂ cup (125 ml) water
1 teaspoon salt

1 Parboil the potatoes for 7 to 10 minutes. Heat the oil in a wok and stir-fry the potatoes for about 5 minutes or until golden. Drain and set aside, leaving the oil in the wok. Stir-fry the onion in the reserved oil until browned, then remove with a slotted spoon and set aside.
2 Dry-roast the cardamom, fennel and cinnamon in a nonstick wok, stirring continuously for 1 to 2 minutes until the spices are fragrant. Drain the soaking cashews or melon seeds, then place in a blender with the dry-roasted spices and grind to a paste, adding 1 teaspoon of water if necessary. Set aside.
3 Stir-fry the ginger and garlic for 2 minutes in the wok used for frying the potatoes and onion, adding more oil if necessary. Add the coriander, cumin, turmeric and red pepper and stir for 1 minute. Leave on low heat while you whisk the yogurt. Add the whisked yogurt, cardamom-nut paste, potatoes, water and salt. Simmer uncovered for about 10 minutes until the potatoes are tender. Stir in the browned onions and serve.

Serves 4   Preparation time: 20 mins   Cooking time: 30 mins

Potatoes with Poppy Seeds and Chilies   Aloo Posta

1¹/₂ tablespoons mustard oil or
  vegetable oil
1 bay leaf
¹/₂ lb (250 g) potatoes, peeled and
  cubed
¹/₂ teaspoon ground turmeric
¹/₂ teaspoon ground red pepper
2 green chilies, deseeded and sliced
¹/₂ cup (75 g) white poppy seeds,
  soaked in water 30 minutes, then
  ground to a paste
¹/₂ teaspoon salt

1 Heat the oil in a wok and stir-fry the bay leaf and potatoes for 2 to 3 minutes. Add the turmeric, red pepper and green chilies and continue stirring for 1 minute. Add the poppy-seed paste, salt and just enough water to cover the potatoes.
2 Cover the wok and simmer for about 5 minutes until the potatoes are half-cooked. Uncover and simmer for 5 to 10 minutes, stirring occasionally, until the potatoes are tender and the liquid has evaporated. Serve with rice.

Serves 4   Preparation time: 15 mins   Cooking time: 20 mins

Spiced Okra Bhindi Bharwan

12 oz (350 g) okra (ladies' fingers),
  washed and dried
3 tablespoons oil
1 teaspoon cumin seeds
1 medium onion, diced
2 green chilies, deseeded and
  minced
$^3/_4$ tablespoon minced ginger
Pinch of asafoetida powder
1 medium tomato, diced

Spice Mixture
3 teaspoons ground coriander
2 teaspoons ground turmeric
2 teaspoons ground fennel
2 teaspoons dried mango powder
  (amchoor)
1 teaspoon ground red pepper
$^1/_2$ teaspoon salt
2 tablespoons water

1 Combine the Spice Mixture ingredients. Cut the stalk off each okra and make a lengthwise slit. Fill each okra with the Spice mixture and set aside.
2 Heat the oil in a wok and stir-fry the cumin seeds for 1 to 2 minutes until they begin to crackle and are aromatic. Add the onion, chilies and ginger and stir-fry until the onion turns transparent. Stir in the asafoetida.
3 Add the diced tomato to the wok, simmer over low heat and stir for 5 to 10 minutes until the tomato turns pulpy. Add the stuffed okra and continue to simmer, covered, for 5 to 8 minutes or until tender and well-coated with the sauce. Serve with steamed rice.

Serves 4   Preparation time: 15 mins   Cooking time: 20 mins

Puréed Mustard Greens and Spinach Sarson Ka Saag

6 cups (1$^1/_2$ liters) water
1 lb (500 g) mustard greens, washed,
  drained and shredded
10 oz (300 g) spinach leaves,
  washed, drained and shredded
2 tablespoons minced ginger
3–4 green chilies, slit lengthwise and
  deseeded
1 teaspoon salt
3 oz (90 g) butter
2 tablespoons fine cornmeal
1 teaspoon ground red pepper
Shredded ginger or coriander leaves
  (cilantro), to garnish

1 Bring the water to a boil in a pot. Add the mustard greens, spinach, ginger, chilies and salt. Reduce the heat to low and simmer uncovered for 10 minutes until the greens are soft. Drain, then purée the greens in a blender or food processor and set aside.
2 Heat 2 tablespoons of the butter in a wok, add the cornmeal and red pepper and stir-fry for 1 minute. Add the puréed greens and the remaining butter, stirring until the greens are heated through and the butter melted. Serve hot, garnished with shredded ginger or coriander leaves.

Serves 4   Preparation time: 15 mins   Cooking time: 15 mins

Fish Pâté in Pastry Blanket Thandi Ajwaini Macchi

Fish goes particularly well with carom, a spice that comes from the same family as cumin and parsley. This elegant recipe from Hyderabad, where European chefs were once employed by the aristocracy, calls for expensive seasonings such as saffron and pistachios and prepares the pâté in a European-style, wrapped in pastry.

Fish Pâté
2 tablespoons whipping cream
Pinch of saffron threads
2 lbs (1 kg) white fish fillets (preferably freshwater), cubed
2 eggs
2 tablespoons butter
1 teaspoon carom seeds (*ajwain*)
2 tablespoons minced coriander leaves (cilantro)
2 tablespoons minced spring onions
$^1/_2$ teaspoon salt
$^1/_4$ teaspoon ground white pepper
1 tablespoon shelled pistachio nuts, skins removed and coarsely ground
Egg wash (1 egg, beaten with 2 teaspoons water)

Pastry
$3^2/_3$ cups (450 g) flour
Pinch of salt
4 oz (125 g) ghee or butter, cut into small pieces
2 tablespoons oil
$^1/_2$ cup (125 ml) iced water

1 To make the Fish Pâté, heat the cream gently and soak the saffron. Remove from the heat and set aside. Place all the Pâté ingredients except the pistachios, saffron and egg wash in a blender or food processor and blend until smooth. Place in a large mixing bowl and stir in the pistachios and saffron cream. Mix well and chill in the refrigerator for at least 1 hour.
2 Prepare the Pastry by sifting the flour and salt into a large bowl. Using a knife, cut the butter into the flour until it is fairly evenly blended, then use your fingertips to rub the butter into the flour until it resembles breadcrumbs. Sprinkle the oil over the flour mixture and use a knife to mix it in. Add a little bit of the iced water and use your fingertips to bring the dough together. Continue adding the iced water until the dough comes away from the bowl in one piece without sticking. Divide the dough into two portions.
3 Using a rolling pin, roll out one portion of the dough so that it is very thin. Shape half of the Fish Pâté mixture into a cylinder, or triangle if preferred, and place in the center of the rolled pastry. Wrap the pastry around the Pâté and apply egg wash on all sides with a brush. Repeat with the other portion of dough and Fish Pâté. Decorate the tops of the pastries with trimmings of dough and brush with egg wash. Bake in a 350°F (180°C, gas mark 4) oven for 30 minutes. Cool, then chill in the refrigerator. Cut into thin slices and serve with Mint Coriander Chutney (page 26) and lemon wedges as an appetizer, or with a salad as a light meal.

Serves 20   Preparation time: 1 hour   Cooking time: 30 mins

Bengali Fish Curry   Macher Jhol

1–1$^1/_2$ lbs (500–750 g) white fish fillets
1 teaspoon salt
1 teaspoon ground turmeric
2 tablespoons minced ginger
Mustard oil or vegetable oil for deep-
    frying
1 large potato, cut into wedges
1 eggplant, sliced
1 large tomato, diced
1$^1/_2$ cups (375 ml) water
2–3 green chilies, slit lengthwise and
    deseeded

Masala
$^1/_2$ teaspoon cumin seeds
$^1/_2$ teaspoon fennel seeds
$^1/_2$ teaspoon black mustard seeds
$^1/_4$ teaspoon fenugreek seeds
$^1/_4$ teaspoon nigella seeds (*kalonji*)

1 Pat the fish dry. Combine the salt, turmeric and ginger and coat the fish fillets well. Marinate for 5 minutes, then cut the fillets into large pieces.
2 Heat the oil in a wok and deep-fry the fish pieces for 5 to 7 minutes until golden brown and cooked through. Set the fish aside, reserving 1 tablespoon of oil. In the same wok, stir-fry the Masala spices for 1 minute until the seeds begin to crackle. Add the potato wedges and sliced eggplant and continue to stir-fry until well-coated with the spices.
3 Place the potato-eggplant mixture and the water in a pot and simmer for 10 to 15 minutes, or until the vegetables are tender. Add the fish pieces and chilies and heat through. Serve with plain rice.

Serves 4   Preparation time: 15 mins   Cooking time: 25 mins

Crispy Fish Morsels Machchi Amritsari

1 lb (500 g) white fish fillets
Oil for deep-frying
$^1/_2$ teaspoon Chaat Masala (page 23)
Pinch of Garam Masala (page 23)

Batter
$1^1/_2$ tablespoons oil
1 cup (120 g) chickpea flour or *besan*
1 egg, lightly beaten
$^1/_2$ teaspoon crushed garlic
$^1/_2$ teaspoon minced ginger
$^1/_2$ teaspoon ground red pepper
1 teaspoon paprika
$^1/_2$ teaspoon ground turmeric
1 teaspoon carom seeds (*ajwain*),
  rubbed slightly with the hand
1 teaspoon salt
1 teaspoon Chaat Masala (page 23)
1 tablespoon minced coriander leaves
  (cilantro)
1–2 green chilies, deseeded and
  minced
2 teaspoons lemon juice
$^1/_2$ cup (125 ml) cold water

1 Prepare the Batter by heating the oil in a wok and mixing in the chickpea flour. Stir for 1 minute, remove from the heat and allow to cool. Mix in the rest of the Batter ingredients.
2 Cut the fish into large pieces, dip them into the Batter and allow to stand for 20 minutes. Heat the oil in a wok and fry the fish for 3 minutes until crisp on the outside and cooked on the inside. Sprinkle with Chaat Masala and Garam Masala and serve hot.

Note: The Batter can be made up to 1 day in advance, then kept refrigerated. Make sure you stir it well before using.

Serves 4   Preparation time: 20 mins   Cooking time: 5 mins

Fish in Coconut Milk   Meen Molee

4 whole small fish, weighing about
   12 oz (350 g) each, or 1¹/₂ lbs (750 g)
   white fish steaks
¹/₂ teaspoon ground turmeric
1 teaspoon ground red pepper
1 teaspoon salt
3¹/₂ tablespoons oil
³/₄ in (2 cm) ginger, sliced
6–8 cloves garlic
3–4 green chilies, slit lengthwise and
   deseeded
6 green cardamom pods, bruised
2 medium onions, sliced
2 teaspoons ground coriander
1¹/₂ cups (375 ml) thin coconut milk
Banana leaf (optional)
30 curry leaves
¹/₂ cup (125 ml) coconut cream or 1
   cup (250 ml) thick coconut milk
1 teaspoon black mustard seeds
1 lime or lemon, to serve

1 Clean the fish and cut slits on both sides to allow the spices to penetrate. Combine the turmeric, red pepper and salt and marinate the fish for 5 minutes. Heat 3 tablespoons of the oil in a wok and stir-fry the fish on both sides for 5 to 10 minutes or until golden brown. Remove and set aside.
2 In the same wok, stir-fry the ginger, garlic, green chilies, cardamoms and onion. Add the ground coriander and the thin coconut milk and stir well. Allow the milk to heat through, cool slightly, then blend to a smooth paste in a blender or food processor.
3 Line the bottom of a wide, thick-bottomed skillet with the banana leaf; this is optional, but adds a delicate flavor to the curry. Place the curry leaves and fish on the banana leaf and pour the blended sauce over it. Bring to a boil uncovered and simmer over low heat for 5 to 10 minutes until the fish is cooked. Add the coconut cream and heat through. Do not allow the coconut cream to boil.
4 Heat ¹/₂ tablespoon of oil in a wok and stir-fry the mustard seeds for 1 minute until they begin to pop. Pour the mustard seeds over the fish and serve with lime or lemon juice squeezed over the top.

Serves 4   Preparation time: 25 mins   Cooking time: 20 mins

Kerala Shrimp Curry   Kanju Masala

2 dried chilies, torn and soaked in
   water to soften
2 teaspoons black peppercorns
1 teaspoon cumin seeds
¹/₂ teaspoon ground turmeric
³/₄ in (2 cm) ginger, sliced
4–6 cloves garlic
1¹/₄ lbs (600 g) shrimp, peeled and
   deveined
1¹/₂ tablespoons of oil
20 curry leaves
¹/₂ teaspoon black mustard seeds
1 small onion, sliced
3 tablespoons tamarind pulp, soaked
   in 1 cup (250 ml) warm water,
   mashed, then strained
¹/₂ teaspoon salt

1 In a blender or food processor, grind the chilies, peppercorns, cumin, turmeric, ginger and garlic, adding just a little oil if necessary to keep the blades turning. Combine the spice blend with the shrimp and set aside.
2 Heat the oil in a wok and stir-fry the curry leaves and mustard seeds for 1 minute until the mustard seeds begin to pop. Add the onion and stir-fry until golden brown. Add the shrimp, stirring for 1 to 2 minutes until the shrimp begin to turn pink. Pour in the tamarind juice, add the salt and simmer for about 5 minutes until the shrimp are cooked.

Serves 4   Preparation time: 30 mins   Cooking time: 10 mins

Curried Crabs with Coconut Nandu Kari

This dish comes from Mangalore, on the southwest coast, an area renowned for its appreciation of both fish and coconuts. This succulent curry uses coconut milk plus freshly grated coconut for a wonderfully rich sauce.

3–4 lbs (1$\frac{1}{2}$–2 kgs) fresh crabs
2 tablespoons oil
1 teaspoon black mustard seeds
30 curry leaves
2 bay leaves
3 green chilies, halved lengthwise
Pinch of asafoetida powder
3 medium onions, diced
3 cloves garlic, minced
$\frac{1}{2}$ tablespoon minced ginger
$\frac{1}{4}$ teaspoon ground turmeric
1–2 teaspoons ground red pepper
3 medium tomatoes, diced
1 cup (250 ml) thick coconut milk
$\frac{1}{4}$ teaspoon salt
$\frac{1}{4}$ cup (20 g) freshly grated coconut (optional)

1 Boil the crabs in a large pot of water for 2 to 3 minutes, drain, then cool. Remove the shell of each crab by holding the bottom of the crab in one hand and using the other hand to pull the shell up and off its body. Set aside the shell and discard the feathery gills on either side of the body and any green or spongy grey matter. Rinse and scrub the shell thoroughly, then drain. Quarter the crab and crack the claws so the flavors can penetrate.
2 Heat the oil in a wok and stir-fry the mustard seeds for 1 to 2 minutes until the seeds begin to pop. Add the curry leaves, bay leaves and green chilies and stir-fry gently for 1 minute. Sprinkle in the asafoetida and add the onion, garlic and ginger. Stir-fry until the onion is transparent. Stir in the turmeric and red pepper and continue stirring for 1 minute before adding the crab pieces, claws, shells and tomatoes.
3 Cover the wok and simmer for 10 minutes, stirring occasionally. Add the coconut milk and salt and bring just to a boil, stirring constantly. Mix in the freshly grated coconut, if using, and serve with plain steamed rice.

Serves 4   Preparation time: 30 mins   Cooking time: 25 mins

Spicy Fried Fish   Macher Kalia

1 lb (500 g) white fish cutlets
1/2 teaspoon ground turmeric
1 teaspoon salt
4 tablespoons mustard or vegetable
  oil
1 teaspoon black mustard seeds
2 green chilies, slit lengthwise
1 teaspoon ground coriander
1 teaspoon ground cumin
1/2–1 teaspoon ground red pepper
1/2 cup (125 g) yogurt

Masala
2 medium onions, sliced
1/2 in (1 cm) ginger
4 cloves garlic
3 tomatoes, blanched, peeled and
  quartered

1 To prepare the Masala, grind the ingredients to a paste in a blender or food processor and set aside.
2 Combine the turmeric and salt and sprinkle on the fish cutlets. Marinate for 5 minutes. Heat the oil in a wok and stir-fry the fish for 5 to 7 minutes until golden. Remove, drain and set the fish aside. Reserve 2 tablespoons of oil from the wok.
3 Using the reserved oil, stir-fry the mustard seeds and chilies for 2 minutes. Add the coriander, cumin, red pepper and Masala paste and continue stirring for about 2 minutes until fragrant. Mix in the yogurt and stir for about 5 minutes until the oil starts to separate. Add the fish to the wok and simmer over low heat for 5 to 7 minutes until tender.

Serves 4–6   Preparation time: 20 mins   Cooking time: 25 mins

Creamy Shrimp Curry   Chingdi Macher

3/4 in (2 cm) ginger, sliced
6 cloves garlic
1/2 teaspoon cumin seeds
3 tablespoons mustard or vegetable
  oil
1 bay leaf
4 cloves
1 cinnamon stick (2 in/5 cm)
4 green cardamom pods, bruised
1 large onion, diced
4 green chilies, deseeded and
  minced
1/2 teaspoon salt
1/2 cup (125 ml) water
1 lb (500 g) shrimp, peeled and
  deveined
1 cup (250 ml) thick coconut milk
1/2 teaspoon sugar (optional)
Minced coriander leaves (cilantro),
  to garnish

1 Place the ginger, garlic and cumin in a blender or food processor and grind to a paste.
2 Heat the oil in a wok and stir-fry the bay leaf, cloves, cinnamon and cardamom for 1 to 2 minutes until fragrant. Add the onion and stir-fry gently for 5 minutes before adding the green chilies and the ginger paste. Continue stirring for another 2 minutes. Add the salt and water.
3 Simmer uncovered for 5 minutes, then place the shrimp in the wok and simmer for another 3 minutes. Add the coconut milk and simmer gently for about 5 minutes, stirring occasionally, until the shrimp are tender. Stir in the sugar, if using, and serve sprinkled with coriander leaves.

Serves 4–6   Preparation time: 25 mins   Cooking time: 25 mins

Chicken Tikka   Murgh Tikka

3 teaspoons crushed garlic
2 teaspoons grated ginger
2 teaspoons chili paste or minced fresh chilies
$1^1/_2$ tablespoons oil
$^1/_4$ cup (60 ml) lemon juice
1 teaspoon salt
1 teaspoon Garam Masala (page 23)
Few drops of red food coloring (optional)
1 lb (500 g) boneless chicken leg, cubed
1 cup (250 g) hung yogurt (page 21)

1 Combine the garlic, ginger, chili paste, oil, lemon juice, salt, Garam Masala and red food coloring, if using. Rub the marinade thoroughly onto the chicken pieces. Mix with the yogurt and leave to marinate in the refrigerator for 4 hours (preferably overnight).
2 Thread the chicken onto skewers and brush with additional oil. Place under a very hot grill or broiler for 6–8 minutes, turning once, until cooked and golden brown. Serve with Mint Coriander Chutney (page 26), onion rings, lemon wedges and Indian bread such as Tandoori Naan (page 39).

Serves 4   Preparation time: 10 mins + 4 hours marinating time
Cooking time: 10 mins

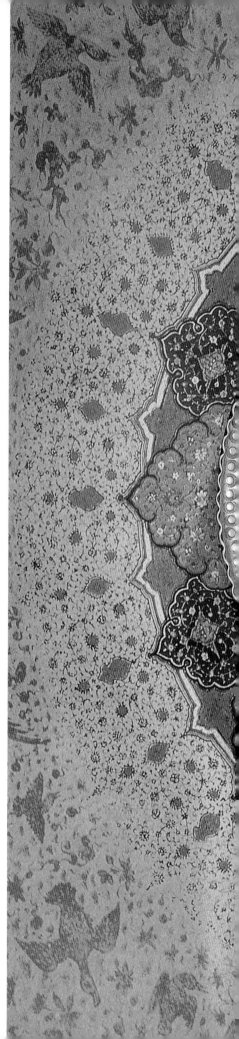

Tandoori Chicken Murgh Tandoori

Originally from the northwest of India, food baked in a tandoor or clay oven, heated with charcoal, is very popular in restaurants all over the country. Marinated chicken cooked in a tandoor achieves an unrivaled succulence and flavor; even when using an electric or gas oven, the result is very good.

2 spring chickens, each weighing around 1^1/$_4$ lbs (650 g), or 3 lbs (1^1/$_2$ kgs) of chicken pieces (legs and breasts)
1 tablespoon chili paste or minced fresh chilies
^{1}/$_2$ teaspoon ground red pepper
^{1}/$_4$ cup (60 ml) lemon juice
1 teaspoon salt
1 teaspoon Chaat Masala (page 23)
Melted butter, to baste

Marinade
2 cups (500 g) hung yogurt (page 21)
1^1/$_2$ tablespoons chili paste or minced fresh chilies (optional)
1 tablespoon crushed garlic
1 tablespoon minced ginger
1 tablespoon oil
1 tablespoon lemon juice
2 teaspoons Garam Masala (page 23)
Few drops of red food coloring (optional)

1 Make deep cuts on the inside (if using whole chickens) and the outside of the chickens or chicken pieces, to allow the Marinade to penetrate. Combine the chili paste, red pepper, lemon juice and salt, and rub onto the chickens. Refrigerate for 30 minutes.
2 Make the Marinade by combining all the ingredients, then rub the Marinade onto the chickens. Save some Marinade to rub inside the chest cavity. Marinate the chickens for 3 to 4 hours or overnight.
3 Preheat the oven to high heat. Place the chickens on a wire rack in a roasting dish, baste with a little melted butter and roast for about 15 minutes until the chickens are brownish-black and cooked. Alternatively, roast on a barbeque for 15 minutes. Sprinkle with Chaat Masala and serve with Mint Coriander Chutney (page 26), onion rings and lemon wedges.

Note: The chickens can be marinated as early as 24 hours in advance.

Serves 4   Preparation time: 15 mins + 4 hours 30 mins marinating time
Cooking time: 15 mins

Mild Chicken Curry Murgh Korma

2 medium onions, diced
4–6 cloves garlic, sliced
1$\frac{1}{2}$ in (4 cm) ginger, sliced
$\frac{1}{4}$ cup (60 ml) water
3 oz (90 g) ghee or butter
4 green cardamom pods, bruised
1 black cardamom pod, bruised
1 cinnamon stick ($\frac{1}{2}$ in/1 cm)
2 cloves
2 bay leaves
$\frac{1}{2}$ teaspoon ground cumin
$\frac{1}{2}$ teaspoon ground coriander
1 cup (250 g) whipped yogurt (page 21)
$\frac{1}{4}$ teaspoon freshly grated nutmeg
1$\frac{1}{2}$ teaspoons ground white pepper
1$\frac{1}{2}$ lbs (750 g) boneless chicken,
  cut into bite-sized pieces
2 tablespoons cream
1 teaspoon salt
1 teaspoon Garam Masala (page 23)
1 teaspoon minced coriander leaves
  (cilantro), to garnish

Nut paste
3 tablespoons white poppy seeds,
3 tablespoons unsalted, shelled melon
  seeds, soaked in water
3 tablespoons *chironji* nuts or
  blanched almonds
3 tablespoons raw cashew nuts,
  soaked in water

1 To make the Nut Paste, first soak the poppy seeds in water and simmer for 30 minutes. Place the poppy seeds and the remaining ingredients in a blender or food processor and grind to a paste, adding water if necessary, then set aside.
2 Stir-fry the onion, garlic and ginger in a nonstick wok until the onion is transparent and very slightly browned. Place in a blender or food processor with $\frac{1}{4}$ cup (60 ml) water and blend to a paste. Set aside.
3 Heat the ghee in a wok, stir-fry the cardamom, cinnamon, cloves and bay leaves for a few minutes, then add the cumin, coriander and onion paste. Continue stir-frying over very low heat, stirring continuously for 5 minutes until the oil separates. Take care that the mixture does not change color. Add the yogurt and continue to stir for 15 minutes.
4 Sprinkle in the nutmeg and pepper, add the chicken pieces and simmer uncovered over low heat for 10 to 15 minutes until the chicken is tender. Add the Nut Paste and simmer gently for 3 to 5 minutes. Mix in 1 table-spoon of the cream, salt and half of the Garam Masala, stirring well. Remove from the heat and serve with the remaining cream and a sprinkling of Garam Masala and coriander leaves.

Serves 4   Preparation time: 1 hour 20 mins   Cooking time: 45 mins

Butter Chicken Murgh Makhani

1 portion of cooked Tandoori Chicken
  (page 78)
2 cinnamon sticks (1$\frac{1}{2}$ in/4 cm each)
3 black cardamom pods, bruised
3 green cardamom pods, bruised
3 cloves
2 bay leaves
1 can (16 oz/450 g) skinned, diced
  tomatoes
2 medium onions, quartered
$\frac{3}{4}$ in (2 cm) ginger, sliced
8–10 cloves garlic
8 green chilies, sliced
8 oz (250 g) butter
2 teaspoons ground red pepper
  (optional)
1 tablespoon sugar
$\frac{1}{2}$ teaspoon salt
$\frac{1}{2}$ cup (125 ml) cream
$\frac{1}{2}$ teaspoon Garam Masala (page 23)
1 small green bell pepper, finely diced

1 Cut the cooked Tandoori chicken into large pieces, leaving the bones in. Set aside.
2 Place the whole spices, tomatoes, onion, ginger, garlic and chilies in a pot and simmer over low heat for 10 minutes, stirring occasionally, until the tomatoes are soft and pulpy. Remove the whole spices from the pot and purée the rest of the ingredients in a blender or food processor. Strain, return the purée to the pot and add the butter, red pepper, if using, sugar and salt. Simmer over low heat until thickened.
3 Add half the cream and the chicken pieces and simmer for 5 minutes. Stir in all but 1 tablespoon of the remaining cream and half the Garam Masala. Mix in the bell pepper and serve sprinkled with the remaining cream and Garam Masala.

Serves 4–6   Preparation time: 15 mins   Cooking time: 35 mins

Saffron Chicken   Kesari Murgh

2 lbs (1 kg) boneless chicken
1 teaspoon salt
2 tablespoons ghee or butter
1 cinnamon stick (3 in/8 cm)
4 green cardamom pods, bruised
3 whole cloves
8 oz (250 g) onions, peeled, boiled,
  then puréed in a blender
1 teaspoon crushed garlic
2 teaspoons minced ginger
1 cup (250 g) whipped yogurt (page 21)
Pinch of saffron threads, soaked in 1
  tablespoon warm milk for 15 minutes
$2/_3$ cup (75 g) unsalted, roasted
  cashew nuts, soaked in water and
  ground to a paste
$1/_2$ cup (125 ml) cream
Fresh coriander leaves (cilantro),
  to garnish

1 Cut the chicken into large pieces, sprinkle with salt and set aside.
2 Heat the ghee in a wok, stir-fry the cinnamon, cardamom and cloves for 1 minute, then add the puréed onions, garlic and ginger. Continue to stir-fry until the mixture begins to take on some color. Add the yogurt and saffron and leave to simmer for 15 minutes, stirring occasionally.
3 Add the chicken pieces, simmer for 5 minutes, then mix in the cashew nut paste. Simmer for about 10 minutes until the chicken is tender. Add the cream, heat through and garnish with coriander leaves.

Serves 4–6   Preparation time: 20 mins   Cooking time: 30 mins

Rich Chicken Curry   Dum Ka Murgh

$1/_4$ cup (60 ml) oil
3 medium onions, sliced
2 cups (500 g) yogurt
1 whole chicken, weighing about 2
  lbs (1 kg), quartered
1 cup (200 g) mixed nuts (almonds,
  cashews and *chironji*), soaked in
  water and ground to a paste
2 teaspoons crushed garlic
2 teaspoons minced ginger
Pinch of saffron threads, soaked in 1
  tablespoon warm milk for 15 minutes
Few drops rose essence
4 cloves
3 green cardamom pods, bruised
2 bay leaves
1 teaspoon salt
Sliced onions, fried in oil, to garnish

1 Choose a casserole dish or wok with a well-fitting lid. Heat the oil and gently stir-fry the onions until browned. Remove the onion with a slotted spoon, reserving 1 tablespoon of the oil.
2 Place the onion and yogurt in a blender and blend to a paste. Combine the onion paste with the chicken pieces, nut paste, garlic, ginger, saffron and rose essence.
3 Heat the reserved tablespoon of oil, stir-fry the cloves, cardamoms and bay leaves for 2 minutes, then add the quartered chicken and salt. Mix well. Leave to cook over very low heat, or in a 300°F (150°C, gas mark 2) oven for 40 minutes, or until the chicken is cooked. Uncover just before serving.

Serves 4–6   Preparation time: 20 mins   Cooking time: 45 mins

Parsi Chicken Curry Salli Murgh

Traditionally served with deep-fried potato straws, this delicious yet easily prepared Parsi dish is also made with lamb (known as Salli Boti).

2 tablespoons oil
2 medium onions, sliced
1 green chili, sliced
$1/_2$ teaspoon crushed garlic
$1/_2$ in (1 cm) ginger
1 teaspoon ground turmeric
$1/_4$ teaspoon ground red pepper
$1/_4$ teaspoon ground white pepper
$1/_4$ teaspoon ground cumin
$1/_4$ teaspoon cinnamon
2–3 medium tomatoes, quartered
$1/_4$ cup (60 ml) water
1 lb (500 g) boneless chicken, cut into bite-sized pieces
1 teaspoon salt
1 teaspoon sugar
5–6 dried apricots, halved (optional)
2 tablespoons cream
$1/_4$ teaspoon Garam Masala (page 23)
Fresh coriander leaves (cilantro), to garnish

Potato Straws
2 lbs (1 kg) potatoes, peeled and finely shredded
Oil for deep-frying
Salt

1 Heat the oil in a wok and stir-fry the onion until golden brown. Add the chili, garlic, ginger, turmeric, red pepper, white pepper, cumin and cinnamon and continue to stir-fry for 3 to 4 minutes. Add the tomatoes and cook for about 5 minutes until the tomatoes turn pulpy. Place into a blender or food processor with the water and blend to a smooth paste. Set aside.
2 Stir-fry the chicken in the wok for 5 minutes, add the onion-tomato paste, salt, sugar and enough water to cover the chicken. Simmer uncovered for about 5 minutes until the oil begins to separate from the gravy. Add the dried apricots and cook for 5 to 10 minutes until the chicken is tender. Stir in the cream before serving.
3 When the curry is ready, prepare the Potato Straws. Dry the shredded potatoes, heat the oil in a wok until it is very hot and deep-fry the shredded potatoes until crisp and golden. Drain and sprinkle the Potato Straws with salt just before serving to prevent them from becoming soft. When serving, sprinkle the curry with Garam Masala and coriander leaves, and top with the Potato Straws (salli).

Serves 4   Preparation time: 25 mins   Cooking time: 35 mins

Goan Pork Vindaloo

This dish was once carried on sea voyages. No water is used in the preparation and the layer of fat on the top helps to seal out the air and preserve the meat. Vindaloos have traditionally been very pungent, although this recipe should cause just a gentle sweat. Choose pork that has some fat on it.

1¹/₂ lbs (750 g) pork, preferably with
  some fat, cubed
4 green cardamom pods
1 cinnamon stick (2 in/5 cm)
1¹/₂ teaspoons mustard seeds
8 cloves garlic
2–3 teaspoons ground red pepper
4 green chilies
1 teaspoon black peppercorns
1 in (2¹/₂ cm) ginger, sliced
2 teaspoons cumin seeds
1 cup (250 ml) coconut vinegar
2 medium onions, diced
¹/₂ teaspoon salt
1 teaspoon sugar
2 tablespoons *feni* or brandy

1 Cut 1 tablespoon of fat from the pork and set aside.
2 Dry-roast the cardamom, cinnamon and mustard seeds in a nonstick wok or skillet for 1 to 2 minutes, stirring continuously until fragrant. Cool, then place in a blender or food processor with the garlic, red pepper, chilies, peppercorns, ginger, cumin seeds and vinegar, and grind to a thick paste. Coat the pork well with the paste and marinate for 30 minutes.
3 Fry the tablespoon of pork fat until the lard is rendered, then add the onion and stir-fry until golden brown. Add the pork (including any marinade) and salt, and simmer over low to medium heat for about 30 minutes until the pork is tender and the gravy is thick. Pour off the excess oil, then add the sugar and *feni* or brandy. Serve hot.

Note: If you cannot obtain coconut vinegar, use rice vinegar or cider vinegar diluted 1 part water to 4 parts vinegar.

Serves 4   Preparation time: 15 mins + 30 mins marinating time
Cooking time: 30 mins

Spicy Hot Lamb Curry   Maas Kolhapuri

2 tablespoons oil
4 medium onions, sliced
1 teaspoon minced ginger
3 teaspoons crushed garlic
3 teaspoons chili paste or minced
  fresh chilies
1 teaspoon ground coriander
$1/_2$ teaspoon ground turmeric
1 lb (500 g) boneless lamb, cubed
4 medium tomatoes, diced
1 teaspoon salt
$1^1/_2$ cups (375 ml) water
3–4 whole dried chilies, fried in oil,
  to garnish
Finely shredded ginger, to garnish

Masala
$1^1/_2$ tablespoons coriander seeds
$1^1/_2$ teaspoons ground mace
4 cloves
2 teaspoons black peppercorns
1 cinnamon stick (2 in/5 cm)
3 dried red chilies, broken into pieces
1 cup (100 g) freshly grated coconut

1 Prepare the Masala by dry-roasting all the ingredients except the coconut in a nonstick wok over low heat, stirring continuously for 1 minute until aromatic. Cool, then grind to a powder in a blender or mortar and pestle. Add the coconut and pulse the blender a few times to mix well. Set aside.
2 Heat the oil in the wok and stir-fry the onion until golden brown. Add the ginger, garlic and chili paste, stirring for 1 to 2 minutes until fragrant, then add the coriander and turmeric. Continue to stir-fry for 2 to 3 minutes.
3 Place the lamb in the wok and stir-fry until browned. Add the Masala paste, stir for 15 minutes, then add the diced tomatoes and salt. Stir in the water and simmer over low heat for 20 to 25 minutes, stirring occasionally, until the meat is tender. Garnish with fried chilies and shredded ginger, and serve with white rice.

Serves 4   Preparation time: 25 mins   Cooking time: 45 mins

Braised Masala Leg of Lamb Raan Pathani

Baby lamb not more than two or three months old is normally used for this succulent dish, but if baby lamb is not available, a larger leg of lamb can be used. The cooked meat should be so tender that it can be served with a spoon.

1 lamb leg, not more than 3 lbs (1$^1/_2$ kgs)
2 tablespoons oil
6 tablespoons tomato paste
1 teaspoon salt
1 cup (250 ml) of water

Marinade
1 teaspoon crushed garlic
1 teaspoon grated ginger
1 teaspoon chili paste or minced fresh chilies
1 tablespoon oil

Masala
4–5 medium onions, sliced
1 teaspoon crushed garlic
1 teaspoon minced ginger
1 teaspoon chili paste or minced fresh chilies
2 teaspoons ground coriander
1 teaspoon ground cumin
$^3/_4$ teaspoon ground turmeric

Whole Spices
3 cloves
4 green cardamom pods, bruised
3 black cardamom pods, bruised
2 cinnamon sticks (2 in/5 cm each)
2 whole star anise
1 bay leaf

1 To make the Marinade, combine all the ingredients together. Make deep cuts in the lamb so the spices can penetrate, then rub the Marinade over the lamb and leave to marinate for 3 to 4 hours (preferably overnight).
2 To prepare the Masala, place all the ingredients in a blender or food processor and grind to a paste. Heat the oil in an ovenproof casserole dish or pot just large enough to hold the lamb leg. Stir-fry the Whole Spices for 2 to 3 minutes, add the Masala paste and continue to stir-fry for about 5 minutes until the oil separates. Add the tomato paste, salt and water and allow to heat through. Add the lamb leg. Make sure the casserole dish or pot is covered with a well-fitting lid.
3 Cook over very low heat or in a 300°F (150°C, gas mark 2) oven for about 2 hours until the lamb is tender, adding more water if the liquid evaporates too quickly. Turn once or twice while the lamb is cooking. Before serving, place the cooked lamb under a very hot grill or broiler for a few minutes, turning, so that the sauce coating dries slightly. Serve with Indian bread such as Tandoori Naan (page 39) or Chapati (page 36), and rice.

Serves 6–8   Preparation time: 20 mins + 4 hours marinating time
Cooking time: 2 hours 15 mins

Goan Spiced Pork and Liver   Sorpotel

The Goan style of cooking pork involves vinegar and spices as preservatives. Traditional Sorpotel used every part of the pig: the liver, kidneys, tongue, ears and blood. Each household has its own version and the following is an authentic family recipe. *Feni*, a liquor made from cashews, is used in Goa, but brandy can be substituted.

$1^1/_2$–2 lbs (750 g–1 kg) pork shoulder, in one piece
1 cup (250 ml) water
1 teaspoon of salt
1 teaspoon ground turmeric
1–2 teaspoons ground red pepper
1 teaspoon cinnamon
2 teaspoons Garam Masala (page 23)
12 black peppercorns
12 cloves
6 green cardamom pods
4 cloves garlic
2 medium onions, diced
3 medium tomatoes, diced
8 oz (250 g) pig's liver, in one piece
$^3/_4$ cup (175 ml) coconut vinegar, or more to taste
1 teaspoon sugar
2 tablespoons *feni* or brandy
$^1/_4$ teaspoon salt

1 Place the pork, water, salt and turmeric in a pot and boil for 15 minutes. Remove the pork, reserve the liquid and cut the pork into bite-sized cubes.
2 Heat a dry wok and stir-fry the meat until browned (the lard that is rendered from the pork fat should be sufficient to cook it). Drain and set aside, leaving the lard in the wok.
3 Place the red pepper, cinnamon, Garam Masala, peppercorns, cloves and cardamom pods in a blender or food processor and grind to make a thick paste, adding vinegar if necessary.
4 Reheat the lard in the wok and stir-fry the garlic and onions until they are browned. Add the diced tomatoes and cook for 5 to 10 minutes until the tomatoes are pulpy. Add the ground paste and liver and cook for 10 minutes, then add the pork and continue to cook for another 2 minutes, stirring occasionally. Stir in the vinegar, sugar, *feni* and reserved liquid to make a thick gravy. Simmer for 15 to 20 minutes until tender, stirring occasionally. Season with salt. The resultant dish should have a curry-like gravy.

Note: If you cannot obtain coconut vinegar, use rice or cider vinegar, diluted 1 part water to 4 parts vinegar. This dish can be made at least two or three days in advance. Goans insist it tastes better after a few days, when the flavors have had a chance to develop and permeate the meat.

Serves 4–6   Preparation time: 30 mins   Cooking time: 1 hour

Lamb Tikka Kebabs   Maas Ke Tikka

2 teaspoons cumin seeds
1 lb (500 g) boneless lamb, cubed
1¹/₂ cups (375 g) hung yogurt (page 21)
2¹/₂ teaspoons chili paste or minced
  fresh chilies
2 teaspoons crushed garlic
1 teaspoon grated ginger
¹/₂ teaspoon ground mace
¹/₂ teaspoon Garam Masala (page 23)
1 teaspoon salt
1¹/₂ tablespoons oil
2 teaspoons lemon juice
Oil, to baste

1 Dry-roast the cumin seeds in a nonstick wok, stirring continuously for 1 to 2 minutes until fragrant. Allow to cool, then grind to a powder in a blender or mortar and pestle.
2 Prick the lamb cubes all over with a fork. Mix the ground cumin and the remaining ingredients (except the oil for basting) together and combine with the lamb, coating well. Leave to marinate in the refrigerator for a minimum of 4 hours.
3 Thread the meat onto skewers and cook under a very hot grill or broiler for 3 to 4 minutes. Brush the meat with oil, turn, and grill on the other side. Serve hot with Tandoori Naan (page 39).

Serves 4   Preparation time: 15 mins + 4 hours marinating time
Cooking time: 10 mins

Lamb Meatballs in Cashew Almond Gravy   Keema Kofta

1 lb (500 g) lean lamb, cubed
3 green chilies, sliced
1 tablespoon minced coriander
  leaves (cilantro)
1 tablespoon minced ginger
¹/₄ teaspoon ground cloves
¹/₄ teaspoon ground mace
Pinch of Garam Masala (page 23)
1¹/₂ teaspoons salt
2 tablespoons ghee or olive oil
1 tablespoon minced mint leaves
Garam Masala, to garnish

Cashew Almond Gravy
2 tablespoons raw cashew nuts
2 tablespoons blanched almonds
1 heaped tablespoon ghee or butter
3 medium onions, diced
³/₄ teaspoon crushed garlic
³/₄ teaspoon minced ginger
¹/₄ teaspoon ground turmeric
¹/₂ teaspoon ground red pepper
3 medium tomatoes, quartered
¹/₄ cup (60 g) whipped yogurt (page 21)

1 Prepare the Cashew Almond Gravy first. Soak the cashews and almonds in hot water, for 10 minutes, covered, then grind to a paste in a blender or food processor.
2 Heat the ghee in a wok and stir-fry the onion until golden brown. Add the garlic, ginger, turmeric and red pepper and continue stirring for about 5 minutes until the oil separates, then add the tomatoes and cook until they become pulpy. Add the yogurt and nut paste and simmer over low heat for 5 to 10 minutes until the oil separates. If a creamier sauce is desired, purée the sauce in a blender or food processor then return to the wok. Leave the Cashew Almond Gravy to simmer over low heat while preparing the meatballs.
3 In a large bowl, combine the lamb with the chilies, coriander, ginger, spices and ¹/₂ teaspoon of salt, leaving the ghee aside. Place the seasoned meat in a food processor and process until very finely ground. Shape into bite-sized balls. Heat the ghee or butter in another wok and stir-fry the meatballs until browned. Drain the meatballs of half the ghee.
4 Place the meatballs in the Cashew Almond Gravy, cover and simmer for 5 to 7 minutes, stirring gently from time to time. Stir in half the mint leaves and 1 tablespoon of salt. Before serving, sprinkle with the remaining mint leaves and Garam Masala.

Serves 4   Preparation time: 45 mins   Cooking time: 25 mins

Fragrant Lamb Biryani Hyderabadi Kacchi Biryani

12 oz (350 g) boneless lamb, cubed
12 oz (350 g) lamb with bone, cubed
2¹/₂ tablespoons ghee or butter
1 teaspoon cumin seeds
7 cloves
1 cinnamon stick (3 in/8 cm)
3 bay leaves
2 black cardamom pods, bruised
7 green cardamom pods, bruised
3–4 green chilies, slit lengthwise
2 medium onions, sliced
1 teaspoon salt

Marinade
1 cup (250 g) hung yogurt (page 21)
¹/₂ cup (125 ml) lemon juice
1 teaspoon grated ginger
2 teaspoons crushed garlic
2 teaspoons Garam Masala (page 23)
1¹/₂ teaspoons ground coriander
2 teaspoons ground red pepper
¹/₂ teaspoon ground turmeric
¹/₂ cup (25 g) fresh mint leaves
¹/₂ cup (25 g) fresh coriander leaves
   (cilantro)
¹/₂ tablespoon salt

Rice
2 green cardamom pods, bruised
3 cloves
1 cinnamon stick (¹/₂ in/3 cm)
1 bay leaf
1 blade of mace
A few rose petals or 2–3 drops of
   rose essence
2 cups (400 g) uncooked long-grain
   rice, soaked 1 hour and drained

1 To make the Marinade, combine all the ingredients. Coat the meat well and leave to marinate for at least 3 hours.
2 Prepare the Rice by placing the spices and seasonings into a large pot of water and bringing to a boil. Add the long-grain rice and boil rapidly for 3 minutes until just half-cooked, then drain thoroughly. Discard the whole spices and set the Rice aside.
3 Heat the ghee over moderate heat in a wok or casserole dish. Stir-fry the spices for 1 to 2 minutes until they begin to crackle, then add the chilies and onion and stir-fry until the onion is lightly browned. Add the salt and the marinated meat, stir a few times, then pour the Rice over the meat. Heat the wok over moderate heat for 3 minutes, then reduce the heat to as low as possible and leave to cook for 45 minutes before serving.

Note: Vegetarians can use firm tofu in place of the meat, but the tofu needs to be scored first before marinating. Reduce the cooking time in step 3 to 15 minutes, or until the tofu is cooked.

Serves 4   Preparation time: 45 mins + 3 hours marinating time
Cooking time: 1 hour

Meat and Poultry 97

Kerala Lamb Curry   Aatirachi

2 tablespoons oil
6 green cardamom pods, bruised
$^1/_2$ teaspoon black peppercorns
8–10 shallots, sliced
1 lb (500 g) boneless lamb, cubed
$^1/_2$ teaspoon salt
$^3/_4$ cup (180 ml) water
Fresh coriander leaves (cilantro), to
  garnish

Masala
3 medium onions, cut into chunks
$^3/_4$ in (2 cm) ginger, sliced
4–6 cloves garlic
$^1/_2$ teaspoon ground turmeric
2 medium tomatoes, quartered
4–6 dried chilies, broken into pieces
  and soaked to soften
2 green chilies, sliced
6 green cardamom pods
1 teaspoon black mustard seeds
$^1/_2$ teaspoon black peppercorns

1 Prepare the Masala by placing all the ingredients in a blender or food processor, then grind to a paste. Set aside.
2 Heat the oil in a wok and stir-fry the cardamoms and peppercorns for 2 minutes. Add the shallots and continue to stir until they turn golden brown. Add the meat and stir-fry until the lamb is browned.
3 Mix in the Masala paste and stir-fry over low heat for 10 to 15 minutes. Add the salt and water, cover, and cook gently for 20 to 25 minutes until the meat is tender. Garnish with fresh coriander leaves and serve with rice or Paratha (page 43).

Serves 4   Preparation time: 30 mins   Cooking time: 45 mins

Lamb and Corn Curry Makai Gosht

3 tablespoons coriander seeds
2 tablespoons ghee or oil
2 medium onions, diced
2 tablespoons grated ginger
6 cloves garlic, minced
2 cloves
2 green cardamom pods, bruised
1 cinnamon stick ($1/_2$ in/1 cm)
1 blade mace
1 lb (500 g) boneless lamb, cubed
3 green chilies, deseeded and
  minced
1 teaspoon ground turmeric
$1/_2$ teaspoon ground red pepper
$1^1/_3$ cup (200 g) fresh or frozen sweet
  corn kernels
1 cup (250 g) yogurt
1 teaspoon salt
3 tablespoons unsalted, roasted
  cashew nuts, soaked and ground to
  a paste (optional)
$1/_3$ cup (90 ml) cream
Fresh coriander leaves (cilantro),
  to garnish
Finely shredded ginger, to garnish

1 Dry-roast the coriander seeds in a wok, stirring continuously for 1 to 2 minutes until fragrant. Cool, then grind to a powder in a blender or mortar and pestle.
2 Heat half of the ghee or oil and stir-fry the onion, ginger and garlic until the onion is almost transparent. Place in a blender or food processor and grind to a paste, adding water if necessary. Set aside.
3 Heat the remaining ghee or oil and stir-fry the cloves, cardamoms, cinnamon and mace. Add the lamb and stir-fry until slightly browned. Mix in the onion paste, green chilies, turmeric, red pepper and ground coriander. Stir for about 5 minutes until the oil separates. Add the fresh or frozen sweet corn kernels (if using canned sweet corn, add 5 minutes before the end of cooking time), yogurt, enough water to just cover the meat, salt and the cashew-nut paste.
4 Simmer uncovered for 1 hour or until the meat is tender and the gravy has thickened. Add the cream, heat through and serve sprinkled with coriander leaves and ginger shreds.

Serves 4   Preparation time: 30 mins   Cooking time: 1 hour 10 mins

Mixed Lentil, Vegetable and Lamb Stew   Dhansak Dal

This is a favorite among India's Parsi community, who are renowned meat eaters. Dhansak, a mixture of puréed dal, vegetables and meat, is a substantial one-dish meal traditionally served with brown rice, lemon wedges and Kachumber.

1$^1/_4$ cups (250 g) yellow lentils (*tuvar dal*)

$^1/_2$ cup (100 g) red lentils (*masoor dal*)

$^1/_2$ cup (100 g) mung beans (*moong dal*)

$^1/_4$ cup (60 ml) olive oil

2 medium onions, sliced

$^3/_4$ teaspoon ground turmeric

1 teaspoon ground red pepper (optional)

1 lb (500 g) lamb, cubed

1 teaspoon ground coriander

1 teaspoon ground cumin

1 small Asian eggplant ($^1/_4$ lb/125 g), peeled and diced

3 cups (250 g) peeled and diced pumpkin

6 cups (1$^1/_2$ liters) water

1 teaspoon salt

1 tablespoon oil

Masala

1 tablespoon cumin seeds

1 tablespoon coriander seeds

1 cinnamon stick (2 in/5 cm)

5 green cardamom pods

$^1/_4$ teaspoon black peppercorns

8 cloves garlic, sliced

2 in (5 cm) ginger, sliced

7 red chilies

1 Wash the lentils and beans and soak overnight. Drain and set aside.

2 To make the Masala, place the ingredients in a blender or food processor and grind to a paste, adding a little bit of water if necessary. Set aside.

3 Heat the oil in a wok and stir-fry the onion until golden brown. Add the Masala paste, turmeric, red pepper (if using), coriander and cumin, and stir-fry gently for 5 minutes. Place the lamb in the wok and allow to cook for 5 minutes or until all the liquid evaporates.

4 Add the drained lentils and beans, half the diced eggplant and pumpkin, and mix well. Gradually add the water, stirring after each addition, then season with salt and bring to a boil. Cover, reduce the heat to low and simmer gently for 30 minutes or until the meat is tender. Remove the meat and set aside.

5 Purée the lentils and vegetables in a blender or food processor, then return the sauce to the wok. Add the meat, the remaining eggplant and pumpkin, and cook for 20 minutes. Garnish with lemon wedges and serve hot with brown rice and Kachumber (page 27).

Serves 4–6   Preparation time: 45 mins + overnight soaking time
Cooking time: 1 hour 10 mins

Indian Kulfi Ice Cream with Almonds and Pistachios

4 cups (1 liter) milk
$^1/_4$ cup (60 g) sugar
1 tablespoon shelled pistachio nuts,
  skins removed and coarsely ground
1 tablespoon almonds, finely ground
  (optional)

1 Place the milk into a pot and simmer over very low heat. Stir constantly until the milk has thickened and is reduced to about 1 cup (250 ml), or until the milk is the color of the ice cream in the photo (about 1 hour). Stir the sides of the pot constantly to prevent the milk from burning, add the sugar and pistachios and allow to cool. Freeze in individual metal containers such as jelly molds.

Serves 4   Preparation time: 15 mins   Cooking time: 1 hour

Sweet Milk and Chenna Fritters in Syrup Gulab Jamun

6 cups (1$^1/_2$ liters) fresh milk
$^1/_2$ tablespoon flour
Pinch of baking soda (bicarbonate of
  soda)
$^1/_2$ tablespoon shelled pistachio nuts,
  skins removed and coarsely ground
Oil for deep-frying

Homemade Chenna
1$^1/_2$ cups (375 ml) fresh milk
1 teaspoon lemon juice or white vinegar

Syrup
1 cup (250 ml) water
$^1/_2$ cup (125 g) sugar

1 Bring the milk to a boil in a wide, heavy-bottomed saucepan, stirring constantly. Continue to stir over high heat until the milk changes to a dough-like consistency, about 25 minutes. Cool, then crumble the condensed milk solids.
2 Prepare the Homemade Chenna by bringing the milk slowly to a boil and stirring occasionally. Remove from heat and stir in the lemon juice while the milk is still hot, stirring vigorously until the milk starts to curdle. Strain through a muslin or cheesecloth until all the liquid has drained off. Knead the curds lightly until the mixture is smooth.
3 Make the Syrup by boiling the water and sugar together, stirring occasionally for about 10 minutes until thickened slightly. Set aside.
4 Mix the crumbled milk solids with the Homemade Chenna, flour, baking soda and pistachios to form a soft dough. Pinch off a piece of dough to form a small ball—to test the consistency of the mixture.
5 Heat the oil until moderately hot and deep-fry the small test ball; if it breaks apart, the mixture is too moist and a little more flour should be mixed into the dough. When the mixture is the correct consistency, shape the dough into bite-sized balls and deep-fry them, a few at a time, until golden brown. Drain, then place in the warm syrup. Serve warm or at room temperature.

Makes 16 balls   Preparation time: 15 mins   Cooking time: 1 hour

Sweet Yogurt with Saffron   Shrikand

In India, this Gujarati favorite is always served with *puri*. As it is so rich and substantial, you may prefer it simply on its own. If desired, the saffron can be omitted and about $1/2$ cup (125 ml) concentrated mango pulp added for a different flavor.

3 cups (750 g) hung yogurt (page 21)
$1^1/_2$ tablespoons superfine (caster or icing) sugar
1 tablespoon shelled pistachio nuts, skins removed and coarsely ground
1 tablespoon *chironji* nuts, hazelnuts or almonds, coarsely ground
Pinch ground cardamom
Pinch of saffron threads, soaked in 1 tablespoon of hot milk for 15 minutes

1 Sprinkle the yogurt with sugar, stirring until the sugar dissolves, then press the mixture through a fine sieve to obtain a silken smooth texture. Add half the pistachio nuts, the *chironji* nuts, cardamom and saffron (or mango pulp, if using) and mix thoroughly.
2 Chill before serving and garnish with the remaining pistachio nuts or additional saffron, if desired. Serve with Puri (page 36).

Note: If the Sweet Yogurt with Saffron is made a day in advance and refrigerated, the flavor of the saffron and cardamom will be much stronger.

Serves 4   Preparation time: 10 mins

Southern Indian Coconut Dessert   Payasam

Universally popular in the south of India, Payasam is made of sweetened milk with a variety of nuts, *dal*, pearl sago or even wheat-flour vermicelli. This version uses Bengal gram (*channa dal*) and is enriched with coconut milk.

2 tablespoons Bengal gram (*channa dal*) or yellow split peas
1 cup (250 ml) water
1 cup (250 ml) milk
$1/2$ cup (125 ml) thick coconut milk or $1/2$ cup (125 ml) coconut cream
2 tablespoons (35 g) shaved palm sugar or dark brown sugar
$1/2$ tablespoon ghee
1–2 green cardamom pods, bruised
1 tablespoon raw cashew nuts, coarsely ground
1 tablespoon raisins or sultanas

1 Wash the Bengal gram, then simmer with water for 20 minutes until half cooked. Add the milk and simmer for another 20 to 25 minutes, or until the Bengal gram is very soft. Mix in the coconut milk and palm sugar and cook, stirring frequently, for about 1 hour, until the mixture thickens.
2 Heat the ghee in a skillet and stir-fry the cardamom pods, cashew nuts and raisins until golden brown. Add to the Bengal gram mixture. Although Payasam is normally served warm or at room temperature, it can be chilled if preferred.

Serves 4   Preparation time: 15 mins   Cooking time: 1 hour 45 mins

Rich Rice Pudding   Kheer

A northern favorite, this rice pudding is very different from the bland version which countless children had to endure in their homes or boarding schools in Britain.

$1/2$ cup (100 g) uncooked long-grain rice, washed and drained
3 cups (750 ml) milk
2–3 green cardamom pods, bruised
2 tablespoons blanched slivered almonds
Pinch of saffron threads, soaked in 1 tablespoon hot milk for 15 minutes
1 tablespoon shelled pistachio nuts, skins removed and coarsely ground
1 tablespoon raisins (optional)
1–2 tablespoons sugar

1 Place the rice, milk and cardamom in a pot, bring to a boil and simmer gently for 30 to 40 minutes until the rice is soft and the grains start to break up.
2 Add the almonds, saffron, pistachios and raisins, if using, and simmer for 3 to 4 minutes. Add the sugar and stir until completely dissolved. Remove from the heat and serve either warm or chilled.

Serves 4   Preparation time: 15 mins   Cooking time: 45 mins

Cream Cheese Balls in Syrup   Rasgulla

Soft homemade cream cheese or chenna is shaped into balls and simmered in syrup to make a simple but richly satisfying dessert. An extravagant touch in the form of pure silver beaten into the finest possible sheets is sometimes added as a garnish on special occasions in India.

6 cups (1$^1/_2$ liters) fresh milk
1$^1/_2$ tablespoons lemon juice or white vinegar
1 teaspoon flour

Syrup
1$^1/_2$ cups (375 g) sugar
3 cups (750 ml) water

1 Make the Syrup by bringing the sugar and water to a boil. Turn off the heat and set aside.
2 Bring the milk slowly to a boil in a heavy-bottomed saucepan, stirring occasionally. Remove from heat and stir in the lemon juice while the milk is still hot, stirring vigorously until the milk starts to curdle. Strain through a muslin or cheesecloth until all the liquid has been drained off and all that is left are the curds.
3 Combine the curds with the flour and shape the mixture into bite-sized balls. Reheat the Syrup and bring to a boil. Drop the balls into the Syrup, then reduce the heat and simmer for 20 minutes. Add another 2 table-spoons of water to the Syrup every 5 minutes to replace the water lost by evaporation; this is essential to avoid the Syrup becoming too thick.
4 When the cream cheese balls are cooked, about 15 minutes, remove from the Syrup and drain, then cover with water until required. Serve with a spoonful or two of the Syrup poured over the top.

Serves 4   Preparation time: 5 mins   Cooking time: 45 mins

Measurements and conversions

Measurements in this book are given in volume as far as possible. Teaspoon, tablespoon and cup measurements should be level, not heaped, unless otherwise indicated. Australian readers please note that the standard Australian measuring spoon is larger than the UK or American spoon by 5 ml, so use $^3/_4$ tablespoon instead of a full tablespoon when following the recipes.

Liquid Conversions

Imperial	Metric	US cups
$^1/_2$ fl oz	15 ml	1 tablespoon
1 fl oz	30 ml	$^1/_8$ cup
2 fl oz	60 ml	$^1/_4$ cup
4 fl oz	125 ml	$^1/_2$ cup
5 fl oz ($^1/_4$ pint)	150 ml	$^2/_3$ cup
6 fl oz	175 ml	$^3/_4$ cup
8 fl oz	250 ml	1 cup
12 fl oz	375 ml	$1^1/_2$ cups
16 fl oz	500 ml	2 cups

Note:
1 UK pint = 20 fl oz
1 US pint = 16 fl oz

Solid Weight Conversions

Imperial	Metric
$^1/_2$ oz	15 g
1 oz	30g
$1^1/_2$ oz	50 g
2 oz	60 g
3 oz	90 g
$3^1/_2$ oz	100 g
4 oz ($^1/_4$ lb)	125 g
5 oz	150 g
6 oz	185 g
7 oz	200 g
8 oz ($^1/_2$ lb)	250 g
9 oz	280 g
10 oz	300 g
16 oz (1 lb)	500 g
32 oz (2 lbs)	1 kg

Oven Temperatures

Heat	Fahrenheit	Centigrade/Celsius	British Gas Mark
Very cool	225	110	$^1/_4$
Cool or slow	275–300	135–150	1–2
Moderate	350	175	4
Hot	425	220	7
Very hot	450	230	8

Index of recipes

Mail-order/online sources

The ingredients used in this book can all be found in health food stores and markets featuring the foods of India. Many of them can also be found in markets featuring Asian foods, as well as any well-stocked supermarket. Ingredients not found locally may be available from the mail-order or online sources listed below.

Adriana's Caravan
Grand Central Terminal
43rd Street and Lexington Avenue
New York, NY 10017
Tel: 212- 972-8804
www.adrianascaravan.com

A Cook's Wares
211 37th Street
Beaver Falls, PA 15010
Tel: 724-846-9490

Foods of India
121 Lexington Avenue
New York, NY 10016
Tel: 212-683-4419

Gourmail, Inc.
816 Newton Road
Berwyn, PA 19312
Tel: 800-442-2340

Herb 'n' Lore
11 Nadine Ct.
Thousand Oaks, CA 91320

House of Spices
76-17 Broadway
Jackson Heights
Queens, NY 11373
Tel: 718-507-4900
www.hosindia.com

Indian Grocery Store
2342 Douglas Road
Coral Gables, FL 33134
Tel: 305-448-5869

Jyoti
P.O. Box 516
Berwyn, PA 19312
Tel: 610-296-4620

Nancy's Specialty Market
P.O. Box 327
Wye Mills, MD 21679
Tel: 800-462-6291

Oriental Food Market and Cooking School
2801 W Howard St.
Chicago, IL 60645
Tel: 773 274-2826

Pacific Mercantile Company, Inc.
1925 Lawrence St.
Denver, CO 80202
Tel: 303-295-0293
www.pacificmercantile.com

The Spice House
1031 N. Old World 3rd St.
Milwaukee, WI 53203
Tel: 414-272-0977
www.thespicehouse.com

Penzey's Ltd.
3234 University Avenue
Madison, WI 53187
Tel: 608 238-5776
www.penzeys.com

Rafal Spice Company
2521 Russell
Detroit, MI 48207
Tel: 313-259-6373
www.rafalspicecompany.com

Seasoned Pioneers Ltd.
01 Summers Road
Brunswick Business Park
Liverpool, L3 4BJ, UK
Tel: 44-0-151-709-9330
www.seasonedpioneers.co.uk

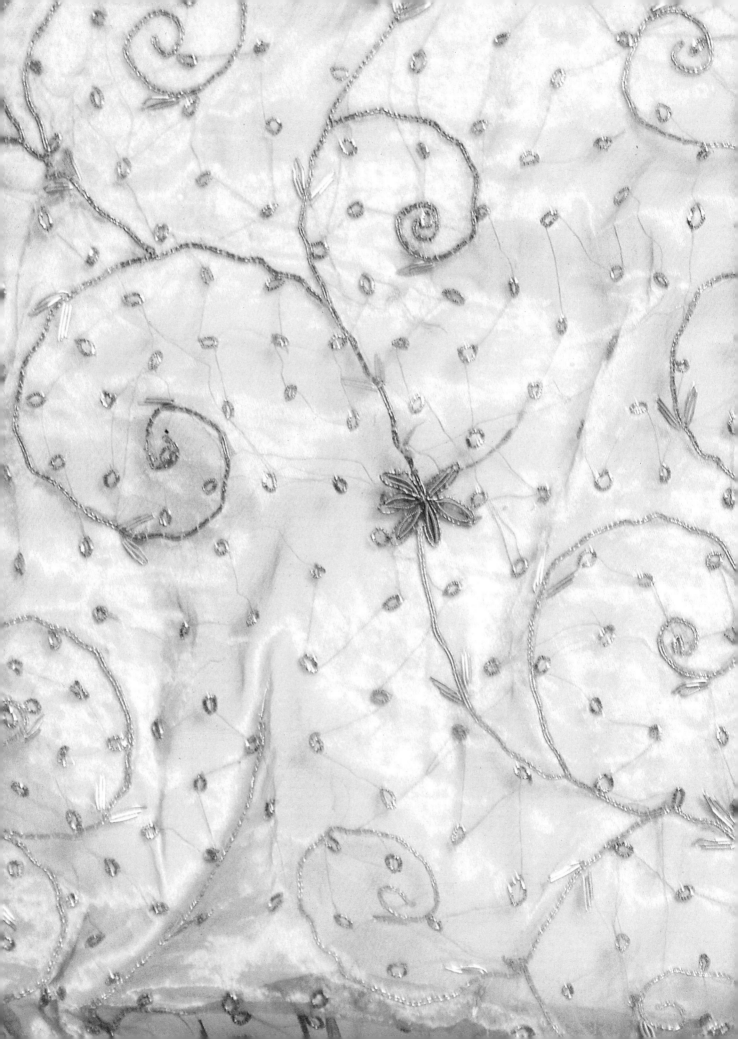